17 Spatulas and the Man Who Fried an Egg

Endorsements

Lisa's simple yet powerful stories will touch you while simultaneously challenging you to look deep within yourself at the "clutter" that is holding you back from being the best version of yourself. We could all be a bit happier if we just tried a LITL.
—**Harry Roberts,** Co-Founder of MattressFirm

A masterful storyteller, Lisa invites us into the spaces of her life and her clients' lives, where intimate untold stories lie buried in disorganized, often cluttered rooms. With compassion and wisdom, she connects with her clients who share their emotional attachment to the tangibles that have become their lives. Offering her clients a simple and sensible four-step model for letting go of "things" that for decades have consumed all the corners of their minds and hearts, she helps them untether from the chaos and regain a sense of order and peace. Refreshing, delightful, endearing, and practical, Lisa's book is about our interior home, the sacred space where all our lived experiences are stored, as much as it is about the sacred space of our physical home. I highly recommend *17 Spatulas and the Man Who Fried an Egg* to anyone ready for a practical, heart-centered guide for decluttering and reclaiming their space and lives.
—**Suzanne Nixon,** EdD, LPC, LMFT, CMT
Psychotherapist, Somatic Therapist, Mindfulness Meditation Teacher

Lisa's book encouraged me to see my belongings in a new light, and when I believed I was too busy, I remembered I intended to clean up my kitchen and living room on the weekend. Imagining Lisa's encouraging voice supporting me made it fun and easy, and I feel so excited to keep going in the other rooms!
—**Lynn Thompson,** Writer and Editor

I've known Lisa for approximately 42 years. Through our occasional visits over the years, I've had the opportunity to see her grow into this incredibly insightful woman, which has been a true blessing and the primary reason I recognize this book. In addition to drawing from her experiences with clients she has guided to "declutter" their living spaces, she shares her own personal "decluttering," both physical and emotional, which interestingly reflects the clutter we all face. When we went through the COVID shutdown, many of us "shut down." I did. But eventually, I started clearing my home of excess "clutter," as recommended by Lisa in this book, and felt my life becoming more open and lighter. If you want a lift in your spirit, brighter light in your eyes, and freedom, here is a huge step to get you there.

—**Kevyn Morrow,** Broadway, Television, Film Actor

Why does our stuff—even our oldest, barely-used, and probably useless stuff—have such an emotional grip on our psyches and, thus, our actions (or inactions)? This emotional straitjacket often reaches the point of absurdity, as we can't bring ourselves to move on from the items that clutter our closets, shelves, homes, and minds. Lisa Geraci Rigoni knows why. She reveals these truths about herself, and in the process, she does the same for her readers, simply by being honest about that visceral vice grip that a simple, inanimate object has over us. With anecdotes about her quirky clients and even quirkier family (is there any other kind?), Lisa takes us on a journey that begins in childhood and informs us how our habits, fears, and obsessions regarding the objects in our lives are rooted in deep human connections. Then, by honestly assessing our ties with the stuff in our lives, we can make sense of why we hold on and how we move on to better caring for what we keep and letting the rest go."

—**Tony Howard,** CCE, IOM
President & CEO, Loudoun Chamber of Commerce

17 Spatulas and the Man Who Fried an Egg guided me in finding ways to embrace the present more by honoring my past and figuring out which things I really needed to represent it and what I could finally release.

—**Billy Wirth,** Award-winning actor, director, producer

By the very title, *17 Spatulas and the Man Who Fried an Egg,* you can expect the unexpected, along with some laughs and maybe some tears. Oh, you thought you were getting a how-to book on organizing? By the end, you'll be on your way to understanding that happiness isn't about having more or the newest, shiniest thing. Instead, it's about being intentional and treasuring what we choose to keep. So, let Lisa's book support you in organizing and healing your life, mind, and heart. This book will bring you peace.
—**Jan Fox,** M.Ed., BOLD SPEAKING, Increase Your Impact

With 17 Spatulas, Lisa Geraci Rigoni shows she truly understands that simply helping a person organize their space is as useful as painting over a water stain. Though both actions lead to a temporary fix, without exploring the root problem, the issue is sure to return. I immediately connected to Lisa's candid stories about her childhood and her own struggles. The client stories she shares are funny, heartwarming, informative, and inspiring. Lisa's book challenges readers to do the work, but in the most loving way. Reading the wonderful examples she provides of people who have achieved great success in tackling their mental and physical clutter despite what seem at first to be insurmountable obstacles made me feel confident that I can tackle my clutter once and for all.
—**Tom Hodges,** Co-Exec Producer of *Intelligence,* Film/TV Producer, Actor/Producer

If you are looking for a gentle deep dive into examining the intersection of your internal and external clutter, *17 Spatulas and the Man Who Fried an Egg* is for you! Lisa allows the reader to connect the past with the present and offers tools that encourage us to give ourselves grace for integration and authenticity.
—**LeslieGrace Craver,** LMSW, Reiki Master, RYT-200
Founder of *Graceful Transition, Honoring Healing & Growth*

Letting go has always been a challenge. Lisa's book helped me realize I can have memories without a physical representation.
—**Walter Tabayoyong,** CEO of Altamero Management, LA

As someone who has downsized twice in five years, *17 Spatulas and the Man Who Fried an Egg: Reclaim Your Space Mentally and Physically* is a must-read for all who struggle with clutter. Reading Lisa's book has motivated me to tackle my storage room with new insights into what I should keep and why I need to let go. I highly recommend this book!
—**Kristina Bouweiri,** President/CEO Reston Limousine

Lisa's discussions are universal in appeal, and her recommendations make *17 Spatulas and the Man Who Fried an Egg* a practical self-help book. We all know someone who needs to clean up their space. Make the most of your possessions, and take fixations out of your life that drain your energy. It's time to simplify. Lisa's book will help with how you choose and may offer solace in other parts of your life. The important things will become accessible, and you may find yourself again.
—**Nikos Linardakis,** M.D., Pres., The Bene Baby Company

17 Spatulas and the Man Who Fried an Egg is an important book, and we'd all be wise to heed its message. Why do we hold onto "stuff" when it no longer serves us? What's stopping us from releasing old habits, beliefs, and material baggage? The moth-eaten clothes we never wear anymore? A negative report card from 6th grade that saps our confidence to this day? The endless pang from a long-ended relationship, leaving us emotionally unavailable for future love? Is it fear? Habit? Procrastination? Or just a total lack of self-awareness? Only you have access to the answers, and if you're ready to clean out your proverbial house, mind and soul, Lisa Geraci Rigoni will be your guide to finding them. She'll ask the tough questions that will get you to the answers you've been long avoiding, enabling you to finally shed the mental and physical baggage you no longer need. Read it. Use it. Allow Lisa to help you rid yourself of that emotional and physical weight that's been slowing you down. You'll come back from your journey with a new lease on life. I highly recommend you read *17 Spatulas and the Man Who Fried an Egg* for the most useful adventure you'll ever take.
—**Adam Rifkin,** Filmmaker, *The Last Movie Star*

17 Spatulas and the Man Who Fried an Egg: Reclaim Your Space Mentally and Physically empowers the reader to think about why we hold on to things and the memories associated with those things, even though we hear that holding on to the past limits our growth. While reading this book, I discovered that understanding the "why" frees us to let go or hold on tighter. Lisa Geraci Rigoni tenderly shares stories about her life journey and those she met through her work, making me feel that I am not alone. I found myself reflecting on my own life through what ended up being familiar scenarios outlined in each chapter, learning more about myself and my connection to others every step of the way!
—**Stacey Metcalfe,** CEO of Morven Park

I'm eternally grateful for your help Lisa, and thanks for writing this excellent book! I highly recommend *17 Spatulas and the Man Who Fried an Egg* to anyone wondering if they have a clutter problem. My motorcycle mechanic told me many years ago not to fall in love with anything that doesn't breathe or bleed. It wasn't until I attended your seminar that I fully understood the depth of my situation. For some reason, I was predisposed to holding emotional value to relatively worthless items. This book is a great reminder to stay vigilant. For example, I recently accumulated three lawn mowers and only one works. My thought pattern was to use the other two lawn mowers for parts in case my working mower broke down. Fortunately, sanity (Lisa's voice) returned, and I promptly disposed of the two broken mowers.
—**Bill McGowan,** Vice President, John Marshall Bank

17 Spatulas and the Man Who Fried an Egg

Reclaim Your Space Mentally and Physically

Lisa Geraci Rigoni

Goodyear, Arizona

First published in the USA in 2023 by Lisa Geraci Rigoni

Paperback ISBN: 978-1-958405-58-1
Hardcover ISBN: 978-1-958405-59-8
eBook ISBN: 978-1-958405-60-4
Library of Congress Control Number: 2023901324

Publishing House: Spotlight Publishing House™ in Goodyear, AZ
https://spotlightpublishinghouse.com
Developmental Editor: Michelle A. Gil
Editor: Lynn Thompson, Living on Purpose Communications
Book Cover: Deborah Haynes Swider and Becky Norwood
Interior Design: Marigold2k
Portrait Photographer: Stephanie Ascari of Stephanie Ascari Photography
Hair Stylist: Tina White, Second Life Salon
Makeup: Meredith Ehler of Meredith Ehler Enterprises
Nails: Paint Nail Bar Loudoun
Wardrobe: Marinna Rigoni

Disclaimer

In this book, you learn intimate details about the people I have worked with through the years. I have changed all the names and altered some details to respect each client's personal information. I decided to use the names of the adults in my close family, in-laws, extended family, and friends to replace my clients' names. Please know I did not associate my peeps with the situations, so it's not an interpretation of them; it's just how well each name fits the story.

Dedication

To my parents, Alice and Tony,
who did their best with what they had,
fed every stray animal they found,
and loved each other deeply and passionately
for over 50 years.

He who conquers others is strong; He who conquers himself is mighty.
—Lao Tzu

Contents

Foreword

As someone who has spent most of his life selling or teaching others how to sell, I've discovered two secrets to success in what many consider the toughest of professions.

The first is the ability to connect with another human being. The simplest and surest way to do that is to search for things we have in common. It could be learning we're from the same generation. Perhaps we were born, raised, or have lived in similar parts of the country – or countries, for that matter. We might have gone to the same schools. Perhaps we played or have an interest in similar sports. Current or past professions might provide a commonality. Military service. Volunteer work. Family. Pets. What we do for fun. Where we vacation. Our passions. In short, we *will* make that connection if we care enough to invest the time. That connection builds a foundation of trust and begins a relationship with that human being.

We solidify the foundation with the second secret, accomplished when we learn the answer to a familiar question: Why did the chicken cross the road? Let me explain. I ask that question in every class I conduct and then record the answers on a flip chart: *To get to the other side,* I always hear. *Because it wanted to,* is another typical response. It was *searching for something different.* For *more food.* In quest of *better opportunities.* There was a *rooster there.* My favorite: it was *running from Colonel Sanders!* For each answer, I respond with some variation of, *"That's a possibility, but not quite what I'm looking for."* Most classes take hours, if not days before someone finally gets it. So, what *is* the answer, you ask? It's simple, yet quite profound: *"We don't know. So, why don't we ask the chicken? It's the only one who knows WHY!"*

Through her work, Lisa has learned the importance of both secrets. And through her book, we can learn how to apply them! We *must* connect.

We *must* get to a person's Why. And we *must* build a relationship. And when we do, we open the door to freedom. Freedom from stuff. Freedom from clutter. Freedom from the physical and emotional baggage we collect on life's journey. Freedom from the things we truly need to let go of – freedom that, in Lisa's words, allows us to *"reclaim our physical and mental space."* I hope you were paying attention – that's BIG!!!

When I reflect on our meeting, one could view it as pure chance, happenstance, or just plain luck. After all, I'm from Texas, visiting family in DC. Through a personal connection, I accept an invitation to be a guest at an exclusive real estate event in Northern Virginia. And in the presence of over 200 high-powered, professional, dynamic, successful women, I notice Lisa. She's the butterfly of the group, fluttering from table to table, interacting with everyone. She's smiling. She's listening. She's hugging. And she's connecting. And I know I *have* to meet this lady!

Lisa must have noticed me too. Whether it was learning I had authored the book *S.M.I.L.E.* (several were given as gifts by the organizers of the event) or the fact that I stood out like a sore thumb (with my long silver hair, casually dressed in jeans, cowboy boots, and shirt and being one of only three men present), Lisa approached me to purchase an autographed copy for herself. That was the beginning of our relationship.

At happy hour afterward, I learned that this lady – who clearly "had her stuff together" – was NOT a realtor. Instead, she was a sponsor of the event and in the business of helping others "get rid of *their* stuff." Our conversation also revealed that she was a blossoming author, and she respectfully asked if I would consider reviewing her manuscript of **17 Spatulas and the Man Who Fried an Egg.** She had me at the title! Would I *consider* it? No. Would I *do* it? Yes, absolutely, yes! And how thankful I am that I did.

I found **17 Spatulas and the Man Who Fried an Egg** to be powerful, heartwarming, insightful, and brilliantly written! I'm sure you will too. Insider tip, upon its release, I will permanently place **17 Spatulas and the Man Who Fried an Egg** on my list of *"Most-Recommended Books to Read"* I provide my students. I'm glad it made your list!

Now it's time to begin. Turn the page and prepare to reclaim *your* physical and mental space!

Steve Rigby
Consultant, Author, Trainer, Speaker

Preface

Do the difficult things while they are easy, and do
the great things while they are small. A journey of a
thousand miles must begin with a single step.
—Lao Tzu

In early February 2021, I was on a weekly call with my marketing team Deborah Haynes Swider and Sharon Wright, co-owners of Loud and Clear Marketing. When I mentioned that I decided to finish writing my book on The LITL System, they were thrilled for me, and Deb told me about a friend who had just started a book-writing group. "Would you like me to introduce you?" Of course, I said, "Sure!" So, we set up a time to talk, and after thirty minutes into the call, I agreed to join the group. Even though it was a significant investment, I knew it was the right way to go since I didn't know the first thing about writing a book, let alone getting it published.

I could never have expected the outcome of that first Zoom call. To start, we each shared about ourselves, the ideas for our books, and our goals for the group sessions. Then, I talked about my business, my team, and what we do for our fabulous clients. My goal was to complete the book and create a workbook to share The LITL System and help more people organize their environments.

The more I talked with my new writer friends, the more stories and questions came up. And the more questions, the deeper we got into the pain of why people have physical and mental clutter. As this discussion progressed, everyone could see that my first book would be less a how-to on organizing and more about the WHY of the struggles that I had uncovered. This book shares my insights into why we hold on to objects, stories, and habits—mentally, emotionally, and physically—when it would be healthier to let go. It's about getting honest with ourselves. Why do we hold on to items, thoughts, and friends that hold us back on so many levels? I realized how many clients I have worked with, how many lives I have impacted, and how they, in turn, have impacted me.

The day following that epic turning point was Wednesday, February 17, 2021, which would have been my dad's 88th birthday, and he inspired me to begin writing and writing and writing. By March 24, over 55,000 words were out of my head and onto the page. Releasing these insights onto paper has been part of the most challenging, exhilarating, and cathartic two years of my life.

I wrote this book based on almost two decades of working with clients and more than five decades of living in my head with myself. When I started telling stories about my clients, wondering where it would lead me, each story led me to another story and another client, which took me back to each of those moments. These stories prompted me to remember and recognize areas where I've held on to resentment, shame, pain, and suffering, related to events, criticism, and stuff from decades earlier.

Growing up with three brothers in a small house in the Chicago suburbs, I was often overwhelmed, so I would find places to get away and calm myself. When I was eight, I created a little refuge in our basement between the wall and my dad's bar that he had built. It was refreshingly cool in the summer, and in the winter months, I would bring my favorite blanket and pillow to keep me warm. Add some of my favorite stuffed animals, games, and books, and I would sneak away and become invisible whenever and for as long as possible. My other favorite place to disappear was my closet, where I would play with my dolls and rearrange my shoes and clothes. That was the beginning of my gift and love of organizing. Although I didn't know it then, it was also the first step in discovering my superpower. A magical way to deal with feelings I had no control over back then was hiding in the hall bathroom and organizing the linen closet, with chaos and disaster just outside the door. Now I realize that I was learning I have the power within me to create a different state of mind by focusing on something other than the uncomfortable situation I found myself in, which always began in overwhelming surroundings.

Going back through my life and being honest and open in sharing these memories and stories with you has been scary, eye-opening, and cathartic. I have become aware of many regrets; some I have learned from, and others still challenge me. I pushed some memories down so deep I had to dig because I wanted to forget most of them. What I didn't expect by going on this journey for you was the avalanche of growth, painful memories, and, thankfully, massive emotional cleansing for me.

Everything I have lived through, including lost dreams and what I thought I would do and accomplish, has brought me to this point. Writing this book has changed and enhanced my perspective on my life's experiences, pain, happiness, and growth, how I talk to myself about my past, and even how I look at things in my home.

Everyone can find stories of regret, lost dreams, shame, and embarrassment, so as you read these stories, I hope you know you are not alone. May they inspire you to change out of your dirty diapers, do the work, and embrace any challenges to letting go. While I'm not a therapist and have no formal therapeutic training, I regularly consult with professionals. I also rely on my intuition. I trust I can make a difference in my clients' lives. Through working with my organizing clients, I found a common thread of holding on and not wanting to let go. It helped me heal, find comfort, and be a better "mentor" and more insightful narrator of our stories.

We all need to hear every word of what the past has to tell us. You are why I wrote this book, to share these stories, examples, and insights for myself and you. Thank you for taking the time to read my book. I hope it helps you. I hope it heals you.

Introduction

One is one too many; one more is never enough.
—Kenny Chesney, musician and singer of "You and Tequila"
written by Matraca Berg and Deana Carter

Why do we keep accumulating and holding on to objects, and when does it become clutter?

I've spent my entire career as a professional organizer contemplating the answers to these questions. I have listened to my clients, both what they have said and left unsaid. After many projects, I would come home, sit down and process my clients' feelings—their agony and challenges when making decisions. I noticed how many of their feelings were similar to mine or another client's situation. The notes I took untapped the power within me to ask focused questions of my clients to make the process of letting go less stressful and more insightful. This book is the culmination of all those lessons and conversations.

Everything we live through, the joys, heartaches, surprises, regrets, lost dreams, and goals accomplished and unachieved, propels us to the next step. This book is different from a how-to for becoming more organized. It is not a "magic pill" that will instantly help you declutter your life. Instead, this book is a memoir of sorts, including my ideas born through my experiences with clients.

You will have to work hard to find your answers to achieve your goals. (Just like anything else in life, right?) You may recognize yourself in one or more of the stories I share. If you do, and even if you don't, after you read it, you will have a choice: put the book up on the shelf with the other "shelf-help" books or make a change. You may finally stop the holding-on-letting-go cycle because you are ready to create a difference in your life.

There is a distinction between reading something and doing something. Most homes I work in have at least one book about organizing on an overstuffed shelf.

Those shelf-help books also add to the clutter and stagnant energy because they represent yet another incomplete goal.

As I tell my clients, I also encourage you to trust. Know that you can declutter your physical space when you recognize why you have been hanging on to the items and what has been holding you back from releasing them.

You will notice I divide the book into four parts based on my proprietary system, The LITL System, which you will learn more about soon.

> *If what you own doesn't help you create the life*
> *you want, why is it in your home?*
> —Peter Walsh, *Let It Go*

I take Peter's quote a step further:

If what you own (hold in your mind) doesn't help you create the life you want, why is it in your home (stuck in your body)? We carry clutter around in our minds, and that mental clutter prevents us from creating the life we want.

For many, the thought of sorting through years' worth of family pictures, memories, clothing, and treasured heirlooms or just plain old "old stuff" is not appealing. Going through takes time and often brings us right back to the time of that picture when your child wore that outfit. The feelings come rushing back, and we are right there again. We can smell it and see it, reminding us of the dreams we once had. We need to keep reminding ourselves that we are not the same person we were and the stuff is just stuff. And we cannot go back. This moment you can choose to move forward.

I wrote this book to mentor, excite, and awaken you—to help you tap into your motivation, power, and confidence. And I'll be here every step of the way.

Remember: You have the power to make the change when you are ready.

Chapter One

Alice Keeps What She Loves

Since I can remember, I've always used the number 17 when exaggerating about anything. So, for years, my elevator speech for the business was, "We can help with all your organizational struggles. From the 17 spatulas in your kitchen, getting your car back in your garage, to a whole house sort, pack, and move."

And then I met Alice.

I've worked in many kitchens over the years, and when space allows, we take out all of the utensils and group them: spoons, tongs, knives, measuring cups, silverware, and of course, spatulas. Seeing everything laid out in categories makes it easier to decide what stays and goes.

Alice's tiny kitchen was probably built in the 1960s and barely fit a kitchen table. But she excitedly led me straight in, chattering and laughing.

"I would cook all day, every day if I still had the strength. After 48 years in this home, Tony and I are moving to a smaller one. We will be closer to our daughters and grandchildren, which will be wonderful. However, Lisa, the kitchen in this new house is even tinier than this one. I don't know how I am going to survive." She giggled. "And you know every item in this kitchen is going with me. I use it all. I've already told Tony and the girls. And now you know too!" She took a deep breath and exhaled, looking right at me, her eyebrows lifted and eyes filled with hope and determination.

"Yep, now I know, too!" I laughed and reassured her. "Alice, you can take anything you want. Let's look at what you have, and then we can pack it all up to prepare for your new home!"

I cleared a space on the kitchen table. Alice wanted to participate, so she brought over all her kitchen utensils and said, "Okay, that's everything."

I categorized her spatulas first, and I stopped in disbelief. "Okay, Alice," I said, laughing again. "You have seventeen! Seventeen spatulas here!"

Alice gasped and shook her head, salt and pepper curls bouncing around her laughing face. "No, Lisa, that can't be! That's way too many. I don't believe you!"

She joined me at the table and recounted them twice.

A quiet snort from the right interrupted us. Tony, her husband, leaned in the doorway, the sleeves of his blue button-down shirt rolled up, exposing arms, still muscular at 71, crossed over his chest. "I bet she has more hidden somewhere, too," he smirked.

She waved a plump hand at him. "Oh, Tony, go back to your shows and leave us ladies to our work." She turned back to me. "Now, this is just silly." She giggled again. "I had no idea I had that many!"

I laughed with her and picked up the two metal spatulas closest to me. "Tell me about this pair, Alice."

She examined each one, holding them in her hand. "Those two metal spatulas are for my heavy-duty pans." She picked up another one with slits. "Oh, it's the perfect size to serve my lasagna, so I don't get the juice on the plates when I serve it."

"Sounds good," I said. "How about this big oval plastic one? I've never seen one shaped like this."

Alice's face lit up as she talked about her family, her love of cooking, and feeding her family with all the love from within her.

"Oh, Lisa, my grandchildren love my pancakes. I have a top-secret recipe given to me by my grandmother. It's written down, and when I pass, my oldest granddaughter will be the caretaker of the recipe and it will live on in our family. It's not one of those healthy recipes, and that's why it is so delicious. I have Tony lift my extra-long skillet from the bottom of the cupboard, and I make pancakes until the kids burst."

She smiled, her eyes lighting up with a love that made me feel nostalgic for my mother's cooking.

"My mom and my Italian and Polish grandmothers loved to cook and were great cooks, so I have been around many a spatula, let me tell you. I seem to recall that my hind end has felt a couple, too!"

And so, the discussion continued. Helping Alice decide which spatulas she wanted to keep that day was so enjoyable. Alice loved to describe the different uses of each spatula. The long skinny one was for a delicate pastry creation with phyllo dough. The round edge was for her homemade crepes. The rubber one that resembled a ladle was for her homemade perogies, ravioli, and tortellini. "You need to be gentle and take them out of the boiling water in perfectly timed precision." She winked. "Now, this one. This one, Lisa, is the best."

I turned to look at it, took a quick inhale, and felt my eyes tear up. "Oh, Alice, that looks exactly like one my mom used to use. I think one of my brothers still has it and uses it."

One corner was melted, like an ear-flapped page in a book. She used this one so often and always held it at the same angle on the hot pan. "See this wooden handle? They don't make them like this anymore. But the handle was too long, so my Tony whittled it down to fit perfectly into my fat little hand." She looked over at Tony, who had been lovingly watching her the whole time. They sent each other an air kiss and a little wink.

Alice became thoughtful as she focused on which spatulas to keep out of the 17 we found that day.

"What about the other nine?" I asked.

"Get those out of the house soon before anyone sees."

I raised my eyebrows. I was confused.

She leaned in with a whisper. "All nine of those are new ones the kids gave me as presents. They want me to replace my 'old, worn out, and ugly' ones." She laughed. "They aren't as good. They're not sturdy and don't feel right in my hand. My life has been about serving my Tony, my kids, and now my grandbabies. It's what I still live for now. Loving, baking, cooking, and keeping them cozy is how I give of myself. I don't need more than what I have used for years. I keep the things that make me happy and feel good."

Alice taught me happiness isn't about having more or the newest, shiniest thing. Instead, what is important is being intentional and treasuring what we have, what we keep, and what makes us feel at home and safe. Even if the spatula is burnt or the finish has rubbed off, what matters is that it feels good in your hand, no matter what it looks like to anyone else. I will always remember the tenderness Alice radiated for her family and her honesty and insight into what brings her happiness. And, of course, her 17 spatulas.

17
Spatulas

Chapter Two

A Universal Theme

By thought, the thing you want is brought to you, by action you receive it.
Whatever your action is to be, it is evident that you must act now.
—Wallace Wattles

Five years into my organizing career, I recognized a universal theme around holding on and letting go: physical clutter often accompanies mental or emotional clutter. Many of us have an intense fear that if we get rid of an object, we somehow disrespect the person, their legacy, and events connected with that object. As a result, we struggle with making mistakes in choices that we may later regret. It was Florence's story that first made me realize this theme.

My realtor friend, Sharon, introduced me to Florence and her son, Peter. Peter and Sharon had gone to high school together in Ohio, where they grew up. He was in Virginia to help her after a fall and was disturbed by the state of her house. He contacted Sharon for guidance.

A few days after our initial phone consultation, we met on a Monday and did the walk through of the white, clapboard townhouse. Immediately, decayed, sour air assaulted my nostrils, and my eyes watered. I left the front door open for ventilation and ventured along a narrow path between stacks of stuff through the first floor.

Peter ran a hand through his thinning, blond hair. "I had to start going through her office and file cabinets upstairs to find papers. We needed information to move her into the rehab center sooner than later."

He winced. "I think I just added to the mess." He continued his story as we picked our way through the cluttered living room. "Florence, my mom, took off when I was five. Dad tried to find her for years, but it was like she had disappeared into thin air. Then, when I was fifteen, we found out she had moved to Virginia, and they were able to divorce. A few years later, my dad remarried, but Mom never did. She's seventy-six, lives alone, and has been in this house for over forty-five years."

His manner screamed discomfort, but I waited for him to get it all out of his system. "I came to visit a few times throughout the years, and she seemed to have so many friends and was very social and traveled a lot, yet I noticed for the last ten years, she was always alone when I would check in." It seemed that a memory caught him, and after a beat, he continued. "The TV was blaring when her neighbor came banging on the door at 3 in the morning. She said the volume had kept her up the night before as well. The doctors think she had been lying at the bottom of the stairs for over twenty-two hours. She fell over all the stuff stacked on the stairs. I don't know how she survived as well as she did."

I looked at him with sympathy and understanding. "Sadly, this story is common. We often work in the home of someone who has fallen or passed away alone, and no one notices for days. It's a good thing the TV was on and alerted the neighbor. It may have saved her life."

Peter nodded. "Thank goodness she only broke her arm."

After finishing our walk-through, we scheduled our first session for two days later.

I was waiting on the front porch when Peter and Florence pulled up in a silver Audi. Florence was a tall, handsome woman with short, silver hair and a colorful personality. The right side of her face carried the yellow and green coloring from her fall the week before, and her right hand and lower arm were in a cast and sling.

Peter tried to help her up the curb, but she shrugged him off with, "I broke my arm, not my leg." Then, he caught my eye, told me to text him when we were done for the day, and left.

"Well, aren't I a sight?" Florence joked as she grabbed my arm firmly with her left hand. I instantly felt comfortable with her and knew this would be an interesting project. She forcefully exhaled as we entered the house. "Well, you seem trustworthy. Let's start decluttering this place. I don't want to spend one more night in that hotel. If my son had his way, he would put me in a senior home tomorrow."

As we stood in the tiny foyer, I asked, "Where would you like to start first?"

Florence immediately turned away. "I need to check upstairs." She led me up to her guest bedroom.

When I entered the room, the first thing I noticed was the large oak desk and the minimal decoration. I pulled out the heavy desk chair for Florence to sit on as she instructed me to open the walk-in closet doors and pull out three large plastic bins.

As I opened the doors, lights went on automatically, and I stood in amazement. This closet was more like a shrine. On every available wall space were team shirts professionally sealed in shadow boxes, group photos, and newspaper clippings showing a much younger Florence. Medals and trophies with bowling pins and bowling balls lined shelves. I turned around to look at her, my eyes filled with unspoken questions.

"Please," she murmured, avoiding my gaze, "just bring the bins to me and open them." So, I brought over three bins filled with more bowling trophies, medals, dozens of sweatshirts and T-shirts, hats and jackets, and pins from every event where she had competed. The third bin she had me open contained photographs meticulously arranged in photo albums organized by year and a large stack of letters wrapped in a faded red ribbon. She asked me to hand them to her. With shaky hands and tears welling up in her eyes, she delicately held them as if holding an injured baby bird and clung them to her chest. Years' worth of repressed emotions spilled out of her like the bursting of a dam. Florence held the precious collection tight and cried freely. After several minutes, she took a deep breath; she looked up at me and said, "That's not a side I've shown to anyone, except—" and she held up the stack of letters to me and thanked me for allowing her the space.

She had filled those bins with more than stuff—they held the library of her life—friendships, careers, lost loves, and dreams of things she hoped would happen. So, seeing that closet, filled with memories, hobbies, and her personal history of what she had hoped for in her life, my brain went to other clients, and the puzzle pieces of that theme started clicking into place.

Florence had all these physical objects representing a story of her past and all the heartache. Before we worked together, she could not let go of the bowling items because they described a younger, more vibrant time in her life that she shared only with close friends. I thought back to previous clients and realized there was a pattern. We all have specific objects that carry deeper stories, explanations, and a more profound emotional abyss.

And because of the meaning we have placed on the objects, we create a story. Unfortunately, we often cannot open a box because of the overwhelming fear and stress. So, what do we do with the boxes and boxes of stuff? We let them sit unopened, creating more unconscious tension in our lives. The best way to begin to conquer clutter is to process those deep and often painful emotions and memories, which opens up the story, and, this time, to read the truth.

After thinking about this universal theme and the emotional connection to objects, I approached some of my referral partners—therapists, psychologists, life coaches, and healers. I asked them, "Am I on the right track about this idea? What is your professional opinion on the depth of pain, regret, and despair associated with why people cannot let go of items and thoughts from their past?" Each one I talked with was fascinated and surprised, realizing it is a recurring theme with many of their clients.

These questions planted seeds, and the growth filled this book with over two decades of picking through piles while honoring the beauty of each client's life. My fascination with these answers inspired me to examine how this theme played out in my life.

It was especially noticeable for my clients over forty-five because they have had time to accumulate more physical items and emotional attachments to them. They have also learned more about their family history and stories.

Florence and I worked together for three months, diligently sorting her belongings. After acknowledging the most important objects from her past, she realized she connected them with great times and memories she would always cherish.

Surprising everyone, Florence decided to sell the townhouse and move to a smaller, more manageable two-bedroom apartment in a local senior community. Her decision to sort through her bins was liberating. By removing the negative energy of her old life, she could let go of her past and create a new chapter. Doing so did not erase all the memories she had accumulated, and it never will. Instead, she was able to sort through and choose what empowered her and brought her happiness. Peter, Florence, and I were thrilled that we had achieved our goal; she was now free to make new memories with new friends in a less-cluttered and safer place.

Chapter Three

My Secret Weapon

Persistence is a secret weapon for everyone.
—Lui Wen

My childhood home was a hub of activity growing up. From as far back as I can remember, my Polish-American mother and Sicilian-American father had an open-door policy for humans and animals, so the neighborhood bikes always littered our front lawn. Even though we didn't have much money, my parents were always very generous, and everyone in the close-knit neighborhood came by our three-bedroom, one-bath brick ranch to sit, talk, have fun, get away, and just be.

My parents built the house in 1965-66 with the help of contractors, my grandfather, his brothers, and his friends. Although it was small, it was sturdy, and my three brothers—two older, one younger—filled it with love, laughter, roughhousing, and *lots* of chaos.

The home is still on that beautiful, tree-lined street, in the suburbs of Chicago, within a block from the elementary school. Here's a snapshot of my block in the mid-'70s: about thirty kids from newborn to high school lived in sixteen homes. We all grew up together, played together, walked to school together, and sometimes trudged through feet of snow together (because there were no snow days in the suburbs of Chicago).

We fought, cried, and celebrated births, graduations, marriages, and promotions. We mourned the loss of family members—human and otherwise. Everyone played sports, and we all wanted to sign the cast when someone got injured. First-born, Drew, choreographed our neighborhood talent shows. My youngest brother, Vic, was in charge of car washes in our driveway and was always getting into something he shouldn't.

And Paul, my older brother by three years, was the daredevil, the creator and builder of anything dangerous, bike and car-related. He and Vic would build ramps and, pretending they were Evel Knievel, try to jump from ramp to ramp. My friends and I would lie down between the ramps to see how many of us they could "fly over." Without adult supervision, it's a miracle no one got seriously injured, broke bones, or worse! (The number is zero, in case you're wondering.)

And then there's me.

Mom was pregnant with me while building the house. From the time I was born until the early '70s, a stinky, diesel exhaust-shrouded bus depot was across the street. By the mid-'70s, the town had upgraded the depot to a strip of storefront businesses that included a dry cleaner, a pizza place, a laundromat, a pet store, and a White Hen Pantry, the first convenience store in the area. We felt like we had hit the jackpot! We could buy overpriced last-minute emergency needs 24/7: milk, bandages, magazines, candy, and pop (what we Midwesterners call cola). And of course, Mom's cigarettes.

When Mom had gone through her one-pack-a-day max, I would run across the street—thirty steps door to door—saying the brand over and over in my head so I wouldn't forget it, "Benson and Hedges, Lites 100 Menthol." Running into the store, I'd hand the signed note from my mom to the clerk, *please sell my daughter two packs of cigarettes.* Then, with the packs in hand, I'd skip back home to continue on with whatever silly project I had been in the middle of—playing Barbies or dress-up, riding bikes, or playing school in the basement with all the kids we could fit.

My dad was the happy-go-lucky, fun dad. He had THE loudest whistle. He created a tune, and when he came home from work, a little after 5, he would stand out in the middle of our street and whistle his little song. We all knew it was time to go home when we heard it. That was our end of the "workday." We could be swinging on the swing set at the schoolyard or in someone's backyard, and we would hear the end-of-the-day whistle. Time to clock out! Everybody said their goodbyes, ended the game they were playing, "See you later," and we all went to our homes for dinner. If it wasn't a school night and the weather was good, or it was summer, we'd all meet out in our front yard about an hour after dinner and chores and play together again until it was dark or the mosquitos got to be too much! We'd play hide-and-seek, Red Rover, try to catch fireflies, or whatever we could to stay outside with each other just a little longer.

My mom seemed to enjoy having the neighborhood safe house. She thrived knowing the other parents entrusted her with the protection and safety of the kids, who could hang out there all day and they would not have to worry.

Although I loved being a part of the action, I would quickly become overwhelmed with too much of everything, which happened more frequently as I got older. Laughing, singing, squealing, and yelling—just kids having fun, but it was so much. And noise, such as little-girl screams that were non-stop and SO high-pitched. They don't know how to talk with an "inside voice," especially when they're outside with friends, having a blast.

And don't get me started on the smells of little boys, and UGH, preteen and teen boys—okay boys, in general—their smells are not easy to shake out of your nostrils. The goal was to stay as far away from my brothers and their friends as possible. Then throw in coconut-scented suntan lotion, freeze pops, candy, snacks, and TANG or Kool-Aid—OH, YEAH! This memory reminds me of the sugar highs and lows we all experienced throughout the day. And, of course, more screaming, crying, laughing, and carrying on.

Perhaps other kids wouldn't be bothered by all this activity, but no one ever taught me self-regulation. Either I was part of the party (the center of attention), or I needed to be alone. However, no one gave me permission or the tools to take time out. Back then, who talked about self-care? I didn't want anyone to think I was selfish. It makes me sad that I had a hard time enjoying some of my childhood because of this struggle and wasn't able to express or explain it to anyone. Or even realize why it was happening to me and me alone.

Added to this fun chaos, my three brothers had a saying, "Leave it to Lisa," which was code for *"I don't want to do that or I can't make up my mind!"* It was also sometimes said with a sneer or a huff, as in, *"Leave it to Lisa; she always wants to be the boss and make all the decisions. So let her take care of it."* So, faced with their indecisiveness and being the only girl, I became the one who took care of things, took control, and made decisions. At first, I thought it was an honor—I had the power (or I thought I did). But, by putting the responsibility on my shoulders, when my decisions didn't go as planned or my brothers didn't like the outcome, they blamed me. There was tension when we were all indecisive; if I didn't get my way, I found it challenging to cope with the internal struggle.

I lashed out, screamed at my brothers and parents, got angry, and ran to my room crying. I acted out aggressively, impulsively, and rudely. At the time, I knew it wasn't healthy or rational, but it was the only way to discharge some of the bone-deep anxiety and chronic stress I was feeling.

Then, years into this toxic behavior cycle, I learned I had a secret weapon—I could slip away when no one was watching (or maybe they were glad I was gone). I needed to let go of my emotional turmoil and intentionally change my situation. I created incredible ways to calm myself amid all the chaos. I would go into my room, fold my clothing, organize my stuffed animals from small to tall, or rearrange my books and albums, so they were color-coded or alphabetized. I loved hanging my clothing neatly in the closet and turning all my games the same way to see their titles on the shelf.

These activities were calming and helped create order and tranquility in my brain. I am certain they helped me to function, live, and "survive." The act of sitting peacefully, envisioning a plan, and executing it, gave me a purpose, a focus, and a way to channel all that frenetic energy.

Weeding the gardens with my mom was a lot like organizing— getting out all the stuff you don't need so you can see what's left. Some evenings, the two of us would sit and talk and pull weeds for hours. I adored my time with her and loved seeing the cleanliness, openness, and peace from pulling up weeds. These two activities, organizing and weeding, probably led me to my favorite way to escape the chaos. I snuck into the hall bathroom, which was the only full bathroom for six people for a long time, locked the door, and turned on the fan to drown out all the noise and the commotion on the other side. (No one ever bothered you when the fan was on.) Next, I cleaned off the sink to have a flat surface for "staging." Then I opened the towel closet. It was narrow with long, deep shelves. I could barely reach the back of the top shelf. To put things away, I brought in a chair or stood on the sink, which I realize now was so unsafe.

Opening that closet door would transport me into my happy place. Immediately, I'd know what I wanted it to look like, what I needed to let go of, and how I could accomplish it. I was very intentional about how I wanted the finished space to look and how I wanted everyone to feel when they opened the door and needed a towel or box of tissues. I pictured my mom smiling her gorgeous smile because she wouldn't have to search for anything. I wanted my family to feel as calm as I did while creating my masterpiece.

I began by bringing all the towels out one by one. Then, I folded and stacked them neatly according to size. The fancy towels for the holidays were my favorites. Mom usually took great care of these, wrapping them in plastic bags for safekeeping; little for me to do. They were soft, used less frequently, and lived on the top shelf. When I had all the towels in their respective groups, I organized them by color, lightest to darkest, and put them back in self-appointed groups. For each towel size, I wrote on a piece of masking tape and attached it to the front of each shelf (in the days before labels and label makers) to make sure my family knew where to find the towel they needed.

Time stood still while I transformed the shelves and finished my project and "therapy." I had no idea how long it had been. Minutes, hours? I wasn't interrupted, and it was my little way of calming myself—I needed it. I could escape. I'd disappear and focus on something other than what was happening on the other side of the door. Finally, once I felt satisfied, I would stand back and admire a closet that was neat, orderly, and under control. Calmer and lighter, I was always proud of the finished product; the exercise also transformed me.

Then, when I completed my organizing project, I would turn off the fan, open the door, and walk back out into the chaos, which could have changed a little or stayed the same. Regardless, since I was in a better state of mind, the chaos didn't trigger or affect me as before, so I could function, and I loved it.

I returned to this practice whenever I was overwhelmed—organizing and bringing order to chaos. It became my secret weapon. Even though I had no idea what to call it, I intuitively knew it was the healthiest way to reclaim my peace of mind and be more functional during those highly stressful days.

It would take a couple of decades before I discovered *why* I always felt overwhelmed. However, when I found out and accepted this discovery, I deemed it my superpower, and that's when my secret weapon proved to be an invaluable tool.

17
Spatulas

Chapter Four

The Leave It To Lisa System (LITL)

*Discipline is choosing between what you want
now and what you want most.*
—Abe Lincoln

When my daughter and I were on playdates, the other moms would eventually start talking about how much clutter was in their houses and how they felt so overwhelmed, couldn't get organized, and didn't know where to start. I would say, "Well, let's do something about it."

Most of my friends would say, "No, you don't want to do this," or "You don't have to help me. I'm just complaining." Sometimes I would beg and say, "Come on, let's do it."

Eventually, they would all agree and say, "Really, you would help me do that? Okay—where do we start? What do we do?" So, we would find ourselves organizing cabinets, cupboards, the basement, and even the garage when the weather was nice, and the kids were playing outside. It always was so much fun—and they loved the results. It's much easier to organize when you work with someone, bounce ideas off each other, make decisions, and talk things through.

In 2008, I was working with Laura, one of my girlfriends, while the kids were playing, and she said, "You're so good at organizing. Why don't you make it a business?"

I just laughed. "This isn't a business! It's just something I`ve been doing for myself for years. I am good at it. I enjoy it, and even better when I can help my friends. It's just fun for me."

I organized for family, friends, and primarily, for myself. Remember, it is my secret weapon—to feel centered and grounded and bring my calm back.

As far as business goes, I was so wrong. I researched and discovered that professional organizing is a real business—and an awesome one!

Following that conversation with Laura, I decided to launch my professional organizing company. Once I started with friends, they referred me to their friends, and I quickly got busy. I worked around my daughter's schedule because I loved being a mom, PTA president, and everything surrounding mommyhood. I had owned a fitness business in Chicago for over a decade, so I knew it was essential to get insurance and become incorporated (a Limited Liability Company, LLC). I would be in people's homes, touching their things, and taking things out of their homes for donation, so it had to be an insured and legal company. And a company needs a name.

That old saying of my brothers, "Leave it to Lisa," made perfect sense. I wanted clients to leave disorganized spaces to me, let me take care of it all, and know they were not alone in their organizational struggles. Today, when I organize someone's home, my goal is the same as it always was for me: to help them find their calm within their chaos, whatever that means to them. We would get through those challenges and decision-making processes together and end up with a cleaner, more organized, less cluttered, less stressful home—and life.

Looking back some 45 years ago, I realize that my method of coping and calming myself was the seed of my proprietary system—The LITL (Leave It To Lisa) System. We help our clients a LITL, reduce their stress a LITL, and get rid of a LITL stuff—sometimes a LOTL. It is the guiding philosophy I created to tackle any project and decision.

The **LITL** System

Let It Go Are you ready to let go of certain items? Start with what you know you don't want or need anymore. That is often the bulk of the job. You can make these decisions quickly because, in your gut, you know you're ready to release them. Clearing this first layer away gives you the confidence and momentum you need for the more challenging decisions, giving you a clear view of what's left: these items are potentially still important.

Be Intentional This step can be emotional because some items have baggage. You examine any guilt or reasons behind why you've kept these things. You ask the tough questions. "Why do I still own it?" "What does it mean to me?" "Is it important enough to me to keep and still create the life I want?"

Transform Your Space At this moment, you reflect on what you've accomplished. You've reclaimed your physical space, and with greater self-awareness and honesty, you've also experienced an internal shift and reclaimed your mental space. This change in perspective transforms how you look at your situation, living area, and yourself.

Love It & Live It! You've identified those items you love and choose to keep in your world, which is now focused and less cluttered physically and mentally. As a result, the space surrounding you is a more authentic representation of who you are, so living within that space becomes uplifting and empowering. You'll love it, and you'll love living in it!

The **LITL System** serves two purposes; I created it to help with *any* organizational project, and I found the practical steps helpful in making *any* decision in your life, big or small.

Want to eat healthier? Want to lose weight? First, you need to **let go** of certain foods that may be causing issues with your gut health or are just empty calories. For example, reduce your sodium, choose fruit over desserts high in refined sugar, and forgo most processed foods, caffeine, and alcohol.

Then you make **intentional** decisions on what you *are* going to eat. Create a meal plan, shop when you aren't hungry, and prepare food ahead of time. Add drinking more water to your day. Try some new recipes, and eat more fruit and vegetables.

Taking those two steps **transforms** you and your kitchen because you set a new goal for yourself and surround yourself with healthier foods. You are on your way to being healthier mentally and physically.

The ultimate goal is to **love it and live it** for the rest of your life and stay strong and healthy.

———————

Now you may say, "Okay, Lisa. I see how it worked with food, but how about a new relationship?"

I was having a glass of wine with my friend Larry, who had divorced a couple of years earlier, and he told me he had a list for his dream husband. "He will be six foot five, look like Robert Downy Jr., drive a Beamer, and make at least $400,000 a year!" He was a firm believer and devotee of visualization, and he swore that he wouldn't settle for anything less than the perfect man this time.

He had gone on many dates with men who fit some of his "must-haves" on the list, but they were, well, just "not good guys."

So, while we were talking, I asked, "What are some of the things in a relationship most important to you?"

He thought for a moment. "Well, as you know, I love animals and do a lot of volunteer work at the local shelter, so he should at least like animals." He sipped his Merlot. "He also has to have a sense of humor and not take life too seriously if he's going to be with me!" We both laughed. "And, of course, the most important thing is that he has to love me for who I am."

I smiled. "So, what can you **let go** of?"

He just looked at me for a moment, then took a breath. "Well, I guess he doesn't *have* to be six foot five. But I do want him to be a little taller than me. And it would be nice if he owned a car, lived in a house, and had a steady income!" After we chatted, he decided to **let go** of things he thought he needed in a man. And then, he made an **intentional** decision about what mattered in his life. He **transformed** his way of thinking. And soon after, he began attracting more suitable men because he was now looking intentionally at the **"love and live** with" type of man. When this book was heading to print, Larry was happily engaged to a man who matched him perfectly—and happened to be five foot nine.

I have tested The LITL System with many friends and the choices they need to and have made: job search, buying a car, "decluttering" friends and relationships, and I used The LITL System when writing this book. It started with a first draft of over 55,000 words, so I had to **let go** of what wasn't needed. I made **intentional** decisions on what to keep in the book, and thus, **transformed** the original manuscript and myself. I hope you **Love it and Live it.**

As you can see, no matter your decision, a LITL help goes a long way.

17 Spatulas

Chapter Five

My Superpower

The truth is, unless you let go, unless you forgive yourself,
unless you forgive the situation, unless you realize that
the situation is over, you cannot move forward.
—Steve Maraboli, *Unapologetically You:*
Reflections on Life and the Human Experience

"You're pregnant!"

Tears of joy and relief (and a lot of anxiety mixed in) streamed down my face. For two years, my husband and I tried to get pregnant.

Our journey began when we lived in Chicago, and I shared our struggle with my close friends and clients from my fitness business. Rob and his wife, Rocky, were clients of mine and also doctors, and they suggested we visit a fertility doctor to get a thorough check-up.

"So, what's going on in your lives these days?" the specialist asked.

I blew out a breath and focused on my hands. "We've been trying to get pregnant for so long. Gene was let go from a great company because we chose not to move to China or Poland to keep his job. And my mom was diagnosed with breast cancer for the second time."

The doctor looked at me kindly, and that proved too much.

I started sobbing.

She reached out and gently touched my hand.

It was so ridiculously comforting.

We left with a prescription for an antidepressant I could take while trying to get pregnant and a plan for many tests and early morning appointments.

The medication helped immediately. It smoothed out all the frayed ends. Then, through the battery of tests I underwent, we found I lacked progesterone. Within a week of that first appointment, under the doctor's care and with the proper medication, we got pregnant on our second anniversary. Giving birth to my daughter at age 37 was hands down the best 25-hour, labor-filled, excruciating day of my life. I pushed naturally until the last hour when my body couldn't push another inch. Or centimeter, as it were. But it was so well worth it.

When we started trying for a second child, I assumed I would get pregnant more easily than the first time. We had moved to Northern Virginia by this point. After seeing a few doctors, enduring batteries of tests, and going through a few unsuccessful artificial insemination treatments, we decided to seek a fertility doctor again. We found a private practice, trusting that this time would be as easy as the last one. However, after two rounds of failed and costly in vitro fertilization (IVF) treatments, we decided to stop trying.

I tell you this story because I believe (and I do not know if this is even possible) that the IVF hormones and drugs were so powerful that they may have affected my brain, which was already compromised. I was different after those two treatments. I was so sad and unfocused, and thought I was going crazy. Later, I researched and learned that IVF's long-term side effects could include reproductive complications and increased anxiety, mood swings, reduced sex drive, and depression. No wonder my self-esteem and confidence plunged! Feeling emotionally, physically, and mentally drained drove me to seek grief counseling. I felt challenged in confidence about my body and its natural abilities. This loss severely tested my roles as a woman, wife, and mother. I only wanted to provide a sibling for my daughter's life, and I could not do that. I was devastated. Additionally, people, even friends, commented that I was selfish for only having one child, for example, "How could you do that to your daughter?" Sometimes it was too much for me to bear.

One day, my daughter was singing, dancing, screaming, or crying, I don't even know what it was, and I gave her a little smack on her bottom.

She turned to me wide-eyed and said through tears, "We don't hit in this house, Mommy."

I remember taking her in my arms, collapsing on the stairs with her, and rocking us back and forth, saying how sorry I was and how much I love and cherish her, and she was right, "We do not hit in this house." I was frightened. I was very, very forgetful. I could not focus. And I needed to focus on my three-year-old daughter.

When my husband was out of town for work, I remember how proud I was at the end of the day when I had fed my daughter, and I hadn't burned down the house. Back then, the small things made a difference—not that those were small things.

After speaking to my therapist, he suggested I work with a psychiatrist since I thought something was seriously wrong with me, and what I was experiencing was more than I could explain. I knew my body.

In the first session with the psychiatrist, he started by asking questions about how I manage things, rest, and relax, whether I can ever focus, and if so, when and on what? Were there any triggers that sent me into panic mode? And had I felt them at any other time in my life?

"Well," I said, "where would you like me to begin? At the very beginning."

"Hmmm, okay," the psychiatrist said. "I would like you to go online and take a test for ADD, Attention Deficit Disorder."

I was skeptical and said, "Okay, not sure why you need me to do that. I definitely don't have ADD."

When I went home, I took the test. The test results came in—I have ADD! But, of course, I did not trust it! It's an online test; how accurate could those be?

When I returned to the psychiatrist, I said, "Here are my test results, but I don't believe I have ADD. How can I be successful and productive, raise a child, and do all the things a 'normal' person can do?" So ignorant. Because back then, my limited knowledge of someone with ADD was that they couldn't function in the real world. They need constant help; they can't do anything for themselves. By that point in my life, I had run two businesses, and until then, I was doing very well, thank you very much. Or was I?

I remember the psychiatrist reached to the shelf and pulled off a book titled *You Mean I'm Not Lazy, Stupid or Crazy? A Self-help for Adults with Attention Deficit Disorder* by Kate Kelly and Peggy Ramundo.

When he handed it to me, I again started bawling right there. See, those were the three words I had used to describe myself since I was twelve years old. How did the doctor know? How did *the authors* know? How was it possible? First, I had to read that book to believe I had ADD. Second, how would I stop believing I was lazy, stupid, or crazy?

I read the book over the next few weeks and dove into my past. I saw many ways ADD had challenged me, from excelling in my schoolwork and impacting my early decisions. I sabotaged friendships and relationships because I lacked trust and confidence in myself. The "not knowing why" I felt so different was by far the worst part. When I was younger, I never understood how it could take me so long to read a page and not remember one word I had read. I would have to go back to the top of the page and read it over and over and over again. It was not easy to retain information if I was sitting and reading. Sitting in a class and watching the instructor talk was painful. It often resulted in a daydream or a zone-out session. My focus just wasn't there. I could focus easily when things interested me, and I was physically active.

After all that deep work, I accepted I had ADD and found peace in that knowledge. I still struggle. Sometimes, when the physical and mental clutter gets too much—what do you think I do? I eat well, get some exercise, and organize, and I rely on my love and acceptance of my superpower—ADD. After all, it is what made me who I am today.

Part I

LET IT GO

Are you ready to let go of certain items?
Start with what you know you don't want or need anymore.

Chapter Six

The Man's First Step

"It's the worst you've ever seen, isn't it?" Vince's voice behind me was soft and so low I almost missed his embarrassed words. I stood in the little foyer, packages and stuff piled high on either side. To my left were two steps up to a small half bath; in front of me was a narrow path through the living room. I took a deep breath through my mouth, struggling to dissipate the heaviness in my lungs, and turned to face my potential client.

When Vince called to set up the appointment in the spring of 2014, his anxiety and fear were palpable through the phone. Following his therapist's advice, he researched organizers for over a year, and then, after putting it off, he finally called me.

"I love to read, and I have a lot of stuff—especially computers and electronics." I heard him swallow hard. His voice was worn, tired, and aged. "I'm just not ready to get rid of the things I love. And since it's just me here now, I know it's time to let go of some of them."

"Want to know the good news?"

"Please," he responded.

"I will not make you get rid of anything you love, want, or need, unless you want me to. We start with what you know you don't want and go from there. Then we look at the stuff that has you thinking you need assistance. Which is why you called me." Even though I couldn't see him, as I spoke, I could tell it was like splashing water on a desert. Vince was soaking up my words.

I heard a long inhale and a slow exhale. "Thank you. That is good news, and it comforts me. I feel there is hope, and I can do this with your help." In our fifteen-minute call, I heard his voice with more light in it for the first time. "How soon can you come over? Wednesday next week?"

"I'll be at your door at 10 am, Vince."

The day before I was to meet with him, my phone rang.

It was Vince, speaking rather quickly. "Hi, Lisa, this is Vince. We spoke last week, and we have an appointment scheduled for tomorrow, and something has come up, so I have to cancel."

"Hi, Vince. Is everything okay? Why do you need to cancel?"

He couldn't find a legitimate reason. "I just don't feel ready to take this on. What is going to happen to my stuff? How will I decide? Where will everything go that I don't want?" He was so nervous and embarrassed about someone seeing how he lived. "I have been walking around here for a week, and I am so ashamed at how I have been living. I truly cannot make sense of it. How could I live like this?" He spoke for a long time.

I just listened and reassured him that, at first, we would only meet and talk some more in person. "You don't need to make any decisions this point, Vince. We can even stand outside your door if you would feel more comfortable. You have already taken the first step and reached out to me. Be proud of yourself for doing that."

Before we hung up, he apologized. "I'm sorry for being so dramatic."

I laughed and said, "I will expect nothing less when I see you tomorrow morning."

I got a nice belly laugh out of him, and with that, the tension left his voice. "I look forward to meeting you, Lisa. Thank you so much for listening to me."

When I arrived the following day and knocked, the door opened, and a tall, distinguished-looking man stood in front of me.

"Oh, I'm sorry, I may be at the wrong address."

"Lisa? Hi, I'm Vince."

"Oh! I'm so glad to meet you!"

The actual Vince had no resemblance to the image of the vocal Vince I had created in my head. Immediately I could see intense sadness and despair in his eyes, much more than I had ever seen in a client. We exchanged awkward smiles. Vince gestured with his arm toward the dimness inside his home as he welcomed me. Since he could not fully open the door, he stepped onto the porch so I could squeeze past him and through the doorway. Once immersed in the darkness, the fresh air instantly became a memory as the stale air stifled my breathing.

With every inch of the space piled high, there was no light. The dank, depressing atmosphere drew down the heaviness in my chest, and I felt overwhelmed. But the brutal agony I tapped into and felt emanating from Vince was the most powerful sensation. It was all having a severe impact on my ability to grasp the magnitude of Vince's reality. What had I gotten myself into? Would I be able to help him?

I immediately focused and managed to channel my mental energy and heart on Vince—why I was there and how we could improve his situation. I reminded myself, like I assure my other clients, to take one step at a time. When I turned around, he launched into profusely apologizing as he had done in advance on the phone with me the previous week.

"It's the worst you've ever seen, isn't it?" he said, his eyes down and his hands nervously rubbing together in an absent-minded motion.

"No, Vince, this isn't the worst I've seen, but I understand that this is the worst it's been for *you*. I promise—" I paused and waited until he looked at me. When his saddened blue eyes looked into mine, I channeled every ounce of positivity and compassion and said, "—I promise this will be the worst it's ever been, and once you and I finish, it will never look like this again. You are incredibly brave and I am proud of you for taking this step, trusting in yourself, and wanting to make a change." That was my first glimpse of his beautiful smile. I smiled encouragingly right back at him as he began the careful tour through his home.

I looked to my right. One step down was the blocked entrance to a den, and I had yet to learn what was in or under all the boxes, papers, and trash in the room; two lampshades were sticking out on each side of what I assumed were a couch and side tables. A massive television on a TV stand stood across from the hidden couch. Towering over me was a plethora of unidentifiable items in addition to roughly three dozen boxes and books, storage racks full of unopened CDs, DVDs, VHS tapes, and stereo equipment peeking out.

Directly across from the den were stairs leading up to the second (top) floor. With every step filled with books and papers, garbage bags, and what I assumed was old mail wrapped in grocery bags, the only way I could walk up there was to declutter first. Nevertheless, I took a tentative step ahead of him on the stairs.

"Please, don't!" His voice startled me. "Not ready to show you that yet. That's where my heart died." He half whispered as he lowered his head and walked past me away from the crowded staircase.

I turned to face him. "Oh, Vince, I am so sorry. What happened?" I instantly regretted the words as soon as they were out. "Vince, I apologize. Please trust that you never have to share anything with me unless you want to and feel comfortable. Again, I am so sorry." I looked down and shook my head at myself.

As he headed toward the kitchen, he stopped, turned, and softly said, "My dreams of a perfect life with my beautiful wife were instantly annihilated when I found out she was cheating on me with my friend. I'm not ready to talk about all of that yet. And I definitely cannot go up there anytime soon. Besides, we can't even get up the stairs."

My heart hurt hearing his words that sounded like the first time he had stated them out loud. I followed his lead again, soon reaching the split path left downstairs and right in the direction of the kitchen. Going right, we passed a small area big enough for a table buried under stacks of papers; stuffed boxes choked the space underneath it. Shelving units lined every available wall space. Next to the table stood two wooden bookcases stacked with books, books, and more books. The shelves, sagging under the weight of the books, were so dirty, dusty, and jam-packed, I couldn't tell the age, but they looked antique, made of heavy wood, intricately carved and detailed. "Vince, how long have you had those bookcases? I've never seen anything like them."

"My grandparents brought them from Poland. My grandfather made them. I've had them forever. They are a mess and I hate to think what my grandparents would say about how I let them fall apart."

I smiled and commented, "Maybe they would be happy you still use them and have kept them all these years."

He mused for a moment. "Maybe. Yeah, I like that," he said as he walked ahead.

A jog left in the pathway between piles of stuff was the kitchen, or what I could see. Turning sideways, we accessed the space full of portable shelves that again lined every available wall, crammed full with boxes of empty containers for organizing and storage beside small unopened appliances. The counters were piled high with items used, unused, and expired, packs of batteries, old mail, and papers, in addition to soda cans, water bottles, and open packages of processed foods—chips, cookies, cereal—staples of a limited diet.

Vince again lowered his gaze. "I haven't cooked or sat down to eat a real meal here for over eight years. It's only me. Why make a big deal out of sitting down and eating? The kitchen is my additional storage room!" He snickered, and he was right. The stove was inaccessible, covered entirely, and barely visible under more boxes, except that the door was open, and he used the inside to store paper towels and napkins.

In the only clear space on the counter sat an elaborate, professional-grade coffee maker and all the fixings to go with it.

I turned with a grin. "Vince, do you like coffee?"

He giggled and answered, "It is one of the four main food groups and a necessity of life. It's the only thing that keeps me getting up every day."

"Vince, another maybe silly question—is your oven off?"

He grinned sheepishly. "Ha, yes. As you can see, I use it for storage now too. It stopped working seven or eight years ago."

Fortunately, Vince still had access to his refrigerator, so, he bought milk, orange juice, bread, processed meats, and cheeses. Stacks of frozen dinners, pizzas, and ice cream were in the freezer. Mostly, he ordered in and lived on takeout, processed foods, and canned goods. Vince only used plastic plates, cups, and dinnerware since he could not access the sink to wash dishes, and the dishwasher was blocked.

After he showed me the kitchen, we carefully retraced our steps and made our way to the top of the stairs going down to where he lived, slept, ate, and worked.

"You go first," Vince said, gesturing toward to top step. "It takes me some time to make it down these days. Knees aren't what they used to be. Especially the new one."

I headed down the stairs, and although there weren't many, they were precarious. A narrow path was visible down the middle of the staircase leading down the steps, around a corner, and then through to a short hallway. Boxes of books and papers towered over me on both sides. No one had cleaned the bathroom effectively since bell bottoms were fashionable, and the door could not close with the folding chair in the way stacked high with dirty laundry. It reminded me of camping to imagine using the restroom.

I waited for Vince to come down.

When he made his way over to me, he pointed to the very stuffed and now narrow hall leading out of sight into the back and said, "This level is where I essentially live." So, we were standing in the fifteen-by-thirty-foot area of Vince's home where he ate, worked, read, and slept.

"Oh, do you practice yoga?" I commented as I noticed the three thin, worn, child-size yoga mats, a rolled-up sweatshirt, and a folding chair beside them.

He cleared his throat and looked down. "That's where I sleep. I use the chair to help me up and down, and I can't find the right pillow, so my West Point sweatshirt works fine."

My heart sank seeing this lovely man in such a sad situation. His sleeping area was surrounded on three sides by books piled half the height of the ceiling, and scattered about on the floor were old food containers with leftovers, dirty plates, cups, and dozens of plastic grocery bags filled with trash. Two filing cabinets, a printer, and workstation joined the shelves of books on both sides of his numerous computers.

As Vince held onto a file cabinet for balance, it was painfully obvious he was utterly exhausted. He lived his inner conversation probably as long as he had been stacking boxes, and this moment was rock bottom. I knew he needed to sit down to continue talking. As I pulled out the worn gray folding chair in front of his many computer screens, I said, "Here, Vince, please sit at your desk." I moved a few boxes off another chair and sat down. Finally, we could sit and chat in his cramped living area. I asked him, "What does your day look like?"

"Well, I'm usually up around 10. I go upstairs, make me a great a cup of Joe and a bowl of cereal, and then I make my way back down to eat. I'll power up the computer and stare at the screen for a few hours until I get hungry. Go back up, throw some food together, come back down and stare some more. Same thing until dinner. But then I treat myself and sit in the comfy chair," he motioned to the tattered lime green and brown plaid armchair, "to watch TV or read, then I snuggle in my patch of a bed. Wake up, and do it all again. Groundhog Day—I love that movie."

As we talked, I learned that he had divorced nine years earlier, which was a long, cruel, and hateful process. He had to put his dog down, and around the same time, he had physical ailments and other traumatic events. Vince was very open about his situation and had keen insight into himself.

"I used to have friends, loved to party, and be around people. When all these things happened, people started taking advantage of me and judging me and my decisions. I didn't know where to turn and who to trust. So now, I just don't trust anyone. I've been through four therapists in ten years. This one now, she gets me, and I feel comfortable with her. I used to be a nice person, good and fun to be around. Now, I stay inside like a hermit."

Instantly, I wanted to protect him, hug him and find all the people who had been mean to him and kick their butts. However, that first day, Vince was so open and ready to make some changes, the extent of which I could never have predicted, and he could not have imagined.

We went back upstairs, and before I left, he addressed the proverbial elephant in the room. "About the top floor." I felt his silence linger in the air—his distress and sadness of heavy, weighted pain looking back at me. Gazing through me, he started softly, "That's where my happiness died." A moment more, and then an avalanche of grief came pouring out. "A future with the woman of my dreams, an amazing career, and my precious little Kita, my German Shepherd who was my best friend way before I married. All taken from me in the blink of an eye." He was sobbing, trying to fight the tears, but it was a battle he would not win. Finally, he could bear no more weight. Holding him up, I cleared a space with my foot as best I could on the bottom step, then guided us slowly to help him sit down on the stair.

The sound of pain, loss, and hardship in his voice was heartbreaking, observable in his slumped posture and how he stared into space before speaking again. He had gone through something so profound that I wasn't sure he was ready to confront the pain. The silence was thick, and the pain was raw, but within minutes his energy shifted. Vince's awareness of the past had lit a fire in him.

Standing up, he wiped away tears with his shirt sleeve and looked me directly in the eye. There was more color on his face than when I had arrived an hour before. He had an embarrassed little grin as I extended my hand.

"You know how to reach me. Call me when you are ready to schedule our first session. Or if you want someone to talk to, I'm here for you."

When he spoke, his voice was more relaxed and animated. "When is your earliest opening?" Vince shook my hand, smiling. He was ready!

Chapter Seven

The Unfillable Void

The consequences of today are determined by the actions of the past.
To change your future, alter your decisions today.
—S.N. Goenka

Deep-rooted feelings of shame and guilt—usually tied to experiences in childhood—are some of the reasons that most of us hold on to our stuff. I know this based on decades of organizing, as well as from my own childhood experience.

My dad was a plumber by trade. He worked at various companies and did whatever he could to make ends meet. My mom was the stereotypical '70s and '80s stay-at-home mom in charge of running the household: cooking all the meals (except for Dad's BBQ and pancake dinners), all things kids, paying bills, making decisions, and, well, life in general.

Aside from her two-packs-a-day habit, her one guilty pleasure was her monthly shopping sprees. She and her best friend Sheila would drive to the JCPenney outlet—not even the real JCPenney—and sometimes I would get to go along, and we made it a girls' night out. We would go out after dinner and shop for hours and hours, picking through every inch of the sale racks. One of my theories about retail therapy is that when we don't need anything, we go right to the sale racks. Am I right? Sometimes we're just trying to fill a void or get a fix, and if we find a DEAL on the sale racks, the high is even higher! Aside from clothes (when my brothers and I were young and kept growing), we never really "needed" more stuff. I think Mom and Shelia just needed to get out of the house, and shopping was the most pragmatic and easy excuse to use. Mom craved that high, and I got addicted too and began enjoying and yearning for it with her. When you shop, overeat, drink too much, or do anything compulsively, you get to a point where you covet that euphoric feeling.

I remember feeling rich and lucky when, after a full night of shopping, we would return home with bags and bags and bags of stuff. For a moment, I could forget that I usually wore hand-me-downs from my cousins. Mom and I would burst into the house like a July 4th parade, proudly showing off our large bags stuffed with who knows what. We would find Dad asleep on the couch, getting much-needed rest, or watching TV with my brothers. And then we'd begin the traditional Fashion Show.

I would come out modeling all the outfits Mom bought me, one after another. Dad oohed and aahed, looking at me with such love in his eyes because I was happy, which made him happy. When we were younger, my brothers would participate in the fashion show but only to a certain age before embarrassment took over.

I remember finding my dad's eyes and seeing joy because his wife was feeling victorious about all the great deals. Then, jokingly, Dad would ask, "What did all this fun cost me this time?" My mom would say, proudly, "Everything would have cost $393, but we saved $258, so it only cost $135." Sale prices equaled "frugality" in her eyes.

As I grew older, I avoided looking directly into my dad's eyes because I intuitively felt his worry and anxiety. Even though my parents lived for today and appeared not to worry about the future, supporting his family was my dad's primary focus. He was full of fear about "What am I going to do now?" while he had a smile from ear to ear. He was cluttered mentally and physically and felt powerless, bound by love, devotion, and dread. And I knew it then and my whole life, which added more stress to my already anxious self.

Mom worried too, but it was different. Even though she did have financial concerns (she must have had shopping spree hangovers tinged with regret or fear), her biggest focus seemed to be on us and our family image, ensuring we didn't look like we were struggling. She hated seeing us go to school, outings, or anywhere in worn-out clothes or shoes. That insecurity was undoubtedly a vestige of her growing up in a broken family in the post-Depression era. So, the house ended up cluttered with a lot of clothes and stuff we often only wore or used once or twice, if at all.

I realize now that as much as my dad loved my mom, he enabled her unhealthy spending behavior. The pattern of enabling is universal. We want to see loved ones happy and not ruffle any feathers. And this is the exact pattern that influences my work.

It doesn't matter whether someone comes from money; I have worked with clients in all financial demographics, and they all have compulsive tendencies. Filling a void is universal, and the amount of money you have doesn't deter you from over-purchasing.

Starting my business has helped me to avoid filling myself up with stuff. Even still, old habits die hard and often rear a nasty head now and then. When I feel stressed or overwhelmed and "need" to fill the void, I get lost in that downward spiral and numb myself with my obsession of choice. However, when I am on top of my game, instead of reaching for my credit card or a carton of ice cream, I look at my surroundings and see what can be changed, and then I change it. If I don't see any outer mess, I go inward and do a little mental decluttering. This practice, along with regular therapy, has helped me become aware of the need sooner and be able to catch it—most of the time.

17"
Spatulas

Chapter Eight

The Someday Syndrome

If not us, then who?
If not now, then when?
—attributed to Robert F. Kennedy

Sometimes I'll say this quote, and I'll change it—a LITL.

"If not you, then who? If not now, then when?" And I'll challenge my clients and ask, "Who will make these decisions? Do you want to make them while you can or have someone else make them for you?" Some clients say, "There's no hurry. I'll decide someday."

When is someday going to arrive?

My adaptation of The Someday Syndrome begins with a question: Why do you hold onto stuff? Because:

> It'll be worth money—*Someday.*
> I'll wear it—*Someday.*
> I'll fit into it—*Someday.*
> I'll give it away—*Someday*
> My kids will want it—*Someday.*
> I'll start up that hobby again—*Someday.*
> I will finish that project—*Someday.*
> I'll get to it—*Someday.*

We all use The Someday Syndrome as an excuse and a justification for keeping things and also not having to make a decision. Ask your kids if they want the stuff that you're saving for them; don't assume they do. I often suggest to my clients that for items their adult kids say they will come and pick up "Someday," put them in a box and give it to them as a holiday or a birthday *surprise!* Get it out of your house and into theirs, and then they get to go through it. Or for friends or kids who say they want items, give them a date to get things out or you'll donate them. While it sounds harsh, it is also helpful in extreme cases.

I love hearing someone say, "Well, someday—" They still have hopes for the item. They think they want it for a purpose, or they may be holding on to the dream of using it again. It has a future in their life. For that reason, I'm excited to find out why.

"So, when was the last time you wore that dress?"

"Oh, that was for my daughter's wedding in 1989. I love the floral pattern and the shoulder pads. It made me feel so good, and as you can tell, I was a lot thinner back then." Marie laughed. "I always thought I would fit into it again and surprise my daughter."

To get to the bottom of The Someday Syndrome and the reason we keep things, we must be honest, look at our future selves, and decide how we want to move forward. In Marie's case, when she sees that mother-of-the-bride dress, she relives her daughter's beautiful wedding day and imagines impressing her daughter by realizing her dream of losing weight. Therefore, in her story, it makes sense to keep an item of clothing for sentimental value.

When we looked through more of her closet, I suggested that Marie try on the clothes she thought she would keep.

"Well, even if they don't fit," she said, "someone else might wear them someday."

I smiled. "Okay, who do you think would want it?"

Marie thought for a moment and then admitted sheepishly, "I can't think of anyone."

I replied gently, "How about we donate it to someone who *can* use them now?"

Sometimes it's best to be brutal—rip off the band-aid.

For example, I worked with Dale, a client in DC who needed to move quickly out of the country for a job transfer.

"We paid $15,000 for that dining room set, and none of the kids want it. Can you believe that crap? And I'm telling you now. I'm not selling it for less than $10,000."

I nodded. "I understand. However, we're trying to get you out of the house in a month and finding the right buyer for that price might be difficult. It's only worth what someone is willing to pay for it right now."

That's not my favorite conversation with my clients, but sometimes I need to do it for their sake.

Tom brought me his grandfather's watch at one of my show-and-tell workshops. "I know it's worth a lot of money. I've been saving it, but since I don't use it and none of my kids want it, I figure it's a good time to see how much it's appreciated and finally sell it and cash in."

I took pictures of the watch, sent it to a watch expert I work with, and shared the information I received back a week later with Tom. "At this point, the watch's value is fifty dollars."

"What?!" Tom barked through the phone. "That's ridiculous. I'm not going to sell it for that—it's worth five times that, at least."

I took a deep breath. "Honestly, I understand why you're upset. It sounds like this watch is sentimental and has meant a lot to you. It reminds you of your grandfather, I'm sure."

There was silence for a moment. Then, in a lower and less abrasive voice, Tom asked, "What do you think I should do?"

I replied gently, knowing what I said next would be difficult for him to hear. "Here are my suggestions. Wear the watch and enjoy it. Or get a nice clear case for it and put it on your shelf so you think about your grandfather every time you see it. Or ask your family again, and then, if no one wants it, sell it for fifty dollars. The only person it's worth anything to is you, and you don't want it."

That was a heartbreaking conversation to have, especially about a family heirloom.

I refer to this experience with Tom when I explain to clients who struggle with The Someday Syndrome, hanging on to items with dreams of making loads of money off an "antique." Enjoy it or sell it. It's as simple as that.

———

Why do we pack things away in bubble wrap, in a box, and cram them on a shelf for safekeeping? We tell ourselves we'll use them SOMEDAY, give them away SOMEDAY, or whatever "someday" justification. Grandma won't mind if you chip or break her china. She intended it to be used and loved. So please use the china. Wear the watch. Love the dress and cherish the memories.

Otherwise, *someday*, you will be gone, and those items, with all the family history and memories, will remain unused, forgotten, and gathering dust in bubble wrap on the highest shelf. The choice is yours to keep and use it, or let it go to someone who will use it to start new history and memories.

> *I'm totally holding on to my past. I live in this big house, all by myself, after the divorce, because I can't let go. I have over 80 photo albums. They are organized and labeled! Yet, honestly, I DO look at them and enjoy them immensely. My house is filled with artwork and furniture and stuff that used to belong to my parents. I loved my mom's crazy whimsical taste in decor. My parents died 18 years ago! I'm definitely guilty of "someday syndrome." I still have a lot of my kids' toys—mostly because I have the space for them. I believe raising my boys was such a happy time,*

and I don't want to let it go. Maybe someday I'll have grandchildren???? I think that for me, I hold onto stuff for the calming and soothing effects. A change could make me feel like I'm getting older.

—A professional organizer friend before she
discovered The LITL System

17
Spatulas

Chapter Nine

Guilt about Gifts

We do the best we can with what we know at the time.
—Tamara Wolfe

Why do we surround ourselves with things that don't make us happy or that we don't even like? Look around your home right now—are you holding onto something you don't want? Maybe you hold on to it because it looks good on the wall, matches an outfit you had years ago, or cost you a lot of money when you first bought it, and now it feels wasteful to get rid of it.

When you give yourself time to think about it and talk it through, you realize you don't want the item. It just looks good, and it matches. I live in a house filled with things that I love or like and want to keep around. Yes, there are things that I don't necessarily like but need—the toilet plunger, for instance! For the most part, however, I surround myself with things and people I enjoy.

Accomplishments, Adventures, & Accolades

Many of my clients have traveled worldwide—some were military and collected items on their travels; others were high executives given presents when they met with foreign companies or made purchases when they were abroad. They have plaques, plates, glassware, and vases all over their house to display their adventures, accomplishments, and accolades.

Unless they are valuable monetarily and we can sell them, most of my clients do not want many of those things to go with them to their new house when they are downsizing. If the item was a gift, some don't even remember who gave it to them.

Our accomplishments are important to us, so we keep many of these items out of a sense of nostalgia and as an ego boost—wanting or needing a tangible sign that our lives count for something. Letting go of these material items does not dismiss the importance of our lives and the experiences we've gone through to get where we are today. These keepsakes served a purpose, representing an incredible life lived, a reminder of who we once were (and still are).

Pauline loved music and won various awards for her piano playing in her teens and twenties. Trophies lined her shelves. She hadn't played the piano in years, yet couldn't bear to get rid of them, so they sat, gathering dust.

"Do you love seeing them?" I asked. "When you look at them, does it make you happy?"

She bit her lip, her green eyes pensive. "Not really. Part of me likes to remember how passionate I was about my music. The other part of me feels nothing but grief and sadness at what was." Her voice soft, Pauline looked down at her hands, bent with rheumatoid arthritis.

"Well, you've already told me you're keeping the beautiful baby grand you taught your kids and grandkids to play on, so how about asking them whether they would each like to have one of your trophies?" I patiently waited while she sat down and took deep breaths. I find it's good to give my clients time to absorb and decide from a calmer place when letting go of things. I smiled as a huge smile appeared on her face.

She decided! She was going to ask.

Life moves on and so should we.
—Spencer Johnson

The need to keep gifts

A friend was decluttering her home office and showed me a box of items.

"What is that?" I exclaimed, holding up an odd-looking bird carving. "This does not look like something you would buy!"

Kelly laughed and then rolled her big brown eyes. "I have no idea who gave me that, but I know it was a gift."

"Holy cats," I said. "Do you even like it? Donate it if you don't want it."

She shook her head and blew out a breath. "But how ungrateful am I?! I'd feel so bad. And I know it was a gift, but I can't remember the occasion or the giver!" She felt that keeping it was the height of friendship, and donating was an unforgivable sin. Where does that guilt come from, I wonder?

Another friend of mine, Bryan, had a similar dilemma to Kelly's, only he knew the gift giver—his mother.

She barged into his apartment with a huge black trash bag, exclaiming, "Honey, your father and I bought this for you. We had the flight attendant store it on the plane with us all the way from India!"

While his mother watched with a beaming smile, Bryan tentatively reached into the plastic garbage bag, bracing himself for what he would find. Pulling out a two-foot-high wooden sculpture of Buddha, its front garishly painted, Bryan looked up at his mother and swallowed nervously. "Uh, thanks, Ma?"

She grabbed it from him and walked around his studio apartment, looking for a place to set it. "I know how much you have been trying to find your spirituality, and I just love what Buddha represents and think this would be perfect for you."

He sighed. "Mom, I think it's great, but I don't have the room, and I'm kind of—"

She spoke right over him. "I searched and searched for the perfect Buddha, and even though it wasn't on sale, I bought it anyway. Because you are worth it, and we love you so much and just want you to be happy." She bustled over to a tall, thin bookshelf. "If we just move all your books off this shelf—" She started ripping books down. Then, setting the sculpture on a cleared-off shelf, she gazed at him with love and triumph. "See, it fits!"

What should Bryan do? If you're like most of us "good kids," you keep all the books off the shelf, and there the gift lives.

And his mom tells everyone about this fabulous gift she bought for her son in India. Because this gift represents something to her, she has a relationship with this gift. It represents her love and commitment to her child's happiness. She provided comfort and a special surprise gift out of the blue for her child. And it was expensive. When sharing her story, she presents who she is as a person who searched and searched for the best sculpture with the perfect colors and how she surprised her son. And the fact that you "just love it and keep it right on that shelf" made all that effort worth it for her.

Now, what would you do with the sculpture? How long does it stay on the shelf?

Let me create four personalities, and the first two are unhealthy:

The Repressed Martyr: Buddha stays right where Mom initially put Buddha, and every time you walk past Buddha, you know it is there, and you have a not-so-calm spiritual feeling. Mom (or Buddha) never intended you to feel that way. Every time you look at it, a bit of a negative vibe goes out into the universe, and it also exists in you, the keeper of the unwanted gift. This feeling places a glitch in your perfectly wonderful relationship, and you don't even know why the relationship has changed until you look at the Buddha again. But you don't want to get rid of it. Why? You don't want to hurt the feelings of the gift giver. They spent money on it, and you feel guilty that you don't like it and don't appreciate their kindness. So, you suffer. What is this Martyr-Dom costing you and your relationship?

The Dishonest Captive: As soon as your mom leaves, you look at Buddha, take him off the shelf, and put him on the highest shelf in your closet or under your bed or somewhere where you hope to forget about it. And then, you do forget about Buddha until the day when Mom comes to visit, and you must remember where he is and put him back on the shelf.

The Appreciative Wit: You keep the Buddha gift and have a constant positive reminder of how much your mom loves you. It's so ugly it's funny. It makes you laugh, and you know your mom didn't buy it to aggravate you—she bought it believing it would make you happy. And as silly as it is, it does.

The Confident One: You say, "Thank you," then you donate it and move on. You enforce boundaries in your relationship, one of the biggest challenges for many of us. If you want to make a change, you need to speak up, say thank you for the thought, and then gently tell them that you don't need physical items. Instead, you prefer to spend quality time with them.

There is no law that says you must like, enjoy, or keep every gift someone gives you. If you were my friend and I gave you a gift you did not want or like, I wouldn't want you to keep it around unless it made you feel happy, loved, appreciated, and positive.

These honest conversations are essential to change your life and live authentically. You can honor people yet still set boundaries and put yourself first.

17
Spatulas

Chapter Ten

The Role I Was Never Meant to Play

When we are no longer able to change a situation—
we are challenged to change ourselves.
—Viktor Frankl, *Man's Search for Meaning*

"When I die, you must take care of the boys and keep them in line. You are the only one who can hold this family together. They will be your responsibility. It's what women do."

I remember my mom standing over me like it was yesterday. I was nine years old; Paul, Vic, and I had been playing kickball in the backyard with a few boys from the neighborhood when my mom called me over to stand on the back porch with her. She had been watching us play. I was covered head to toe in dirt, sweat, and crusted blood from the overly aggressive game we had been playing. I was still out of breath from playing when she spoke, barely above a whisper. The sun seemed to dim at her words.

I just nodded with my eyes wide open. "Okay, Mom, I will do that." My chest ached, and the pressure in my body sank my feet as if I was wearing cement boots. And with good reason. That's a lot of pressure to put on a nine-year-old child. I'd like to believe she didn't mean it to be such a burden, similar to all the responsibility her mom put on her at a young age. But this was BIG. She gave me a role, a familial duty, and a responsibility. Unquestioningly, I accepted then and there because who questioned their mother at that age? And I trusted her to know what was best for me.

By the end of 2014, after my parents had passed away and the grieving had lessened, I recalled my mother's instructions. It stressed me out, and I started wondering what I could do to fulfill my role. Especially considering we were all in our forties and fifties at that point. But I took my obligation seriously. I wanted to be sure I was keeping my family together, and I thought I needed to start making decisions.

Now, that doesn't mean I made all the family choices. But in my head, I was in charge. I felt I was the only one able to do it. The only one making sure everyone was getting along and happy (while often I was crabby and miserable.) If there were a disagreement between any of them, I would work hard to smooth things over. I felt I needed to take on the burden of secrets and hold onto the stress of their lives. Because that is what I saw my mom do.

I figured I would make my mom (and dad) proud by "keeping the family together" until the role didn't serve me—or anyone else.

In early 2017, I began working with a therapist who focused on my need or habit of taking on too much responsibility. Soon I realized that my mother had not intended me to become a prisoner to her fears for the family. And that I would not be letting her down or breaking my promise if I stepped back from the role I had played for most of my life.

Our family dynamic is not unique. Many of my friends and clients have shared stories that resemble mine. There is always a peacemaker, a decision-maker or leader, and at least one or two rebels mixed in. I had always been a blend of the peacemaker, the decision-maker, and maybe a little of the rebel.

Once I learned that no one would die if I let go of my perceived duty, I could re-channel that energy I had wasted on worry and the illusion of control.

I need some order and calm to be peaceful enough to enjoy myself and my family. And sometimes, I still step in to get the ball rolling on a decision we need to make as a family, if it serves a purpose. On the other hand, when we take on roles that never fit us quite right, it is like shoes that are too tight; we keep them because we only need to wear them on specific occasions.

Meanwhile, there comes a time when we need to let go of our obligation to obey—and free us to step out from behind the shadow of someone else's fears and live our lives.

17
Spatulas

Chapter Eleven

The Monster in the Closet

*Clutter is the physical manifestation of unmade
decisions fueled by procrastination.*
—Christina Scalise, *Organize Your Life and More*

Suzi opened the door to her guest bedroom with a flourish. "Every time I look in my guest bedroom, I feel like I can't breathe, and my stomach cramps up. I definitely cannot be creative anymore with this mess. So, I just keep the door closed!" She laughed, but I could see the stress around her beautiful brown eyes.

"And what about when you have guests over? What do you do then?" I asked.

She shrugged. "We don't have many guests anymore. My husband and I both work long hours, and on the weekends, we don't want to clean it out. We would rather spend time with the kids and just relax. Upside, it's cheaper than a storage unit, and it's close by—so when I need something, there is no need to leave the house!"

"I understand. It's one of the reasons I'm in business. Not many people want to organize and clean in their free time. So, let me ask; when you do need something from there, how long does it take you to find it?"

She laughed again, running her hand through her thick, black curls. "Oh my, let's not talk about that! Just yesterday, I was looking for my son's soccer cleats—I remember telling him to just throw them in the guest room before a dinner party two weeks ago! When I finally found them, I spent another hour going through a box of drawings the kids did in kindergarten!"

I've had many clients like Suzi. They keep their spare bedroom and closets filled with the overflow, the extras—things they don't need immediately or with clutter they need to move out of the way when they have company coming. "Hurry, grab a grocery bag and shove it all in. Just jam it in the closet or bedroom." Other times, it's a place to throw anything that doesn't have a home. As a result, those spaces become more like oversized junk drawers.

And until you're ready to open that door, you don't even know what's in the back of the room, where it all began. We think it's "out of sight, out of mind," but every time we throw something in the garage, the basement, or the car, our body and mind remember. So, it's normal to feel overwhelmed, even angry, that we let things get this bad.

I tell my new clients what I told Suzi: "Give yourself a break, take a deep breath, and start."

We all procrastinate. Most of us reach a point where the weight of the stuff hiding behind closed doors outweighs our ability to ignore it. We know that out of sight, it's full, even when we're thinking about something else each time we walk by that space. It is like when we were kids and believed a monster lived in the closet. How much energy did we waste stressing about what was behind the door? Imagining the worst and knowing nothing would take it away.

It's the same concept. The door may be closed, but we focus our entire being on the monster clutter behind it. Even when we're not in the room or near it, the negative energy that comes from disorganization and clutter weighs on our minds, adds to our stress, and may even affect our physical health.

The Energy of Stuff

The energy in our stuff is real, and we feel burdened when we hold onto things for too long or for the "wrong" reasons. Compare it to extra weight—the additional stress on your body, your joints, and your energy.

When you have too much stuff in your home and are carrying that extra weight energetically, it makes it more challenging to clean, keep track of things, get around and be productive, focused, and healthy. Also, seeing too much day in and day out stifles our brains, weighs us down, and keeps us heavy. The brain needs a break to focus. In design, it's called "whitespace."

Energetically, when we have too much stuff plus uncomfortable feelings surrounding it, we can be easily overwhelmed and completely exhausted and not even be aware of why. Surrounding ourselves with this kind of energy is like being wrapped in a binding, keeping us isolated and constricted. It may feel protective and safe, but in reality, it keeps us from being able to make changes, move forward, and live comfortably.

17 Spatulas

Chapter Twelve

Memory Hoarders

Hoarding one's hurts hurts only the hoarder.
—Malcolm S. Forbes

Death can sometimes turn even the most minimalist among us into memory hoarders.

I still have a few of my dad's sweaters and sweatshirts. And I feel close to him when I wear them. They make me happy, and they are so comfy. I put one on when I miss him more than usual and need a little extra love. Because that's what my dad gave me—extra love. Wearing his sweaters and sweatshirts makes me feel like he's there, giving me a big hug.

What's the meaning behind the items we hold on to, anyway? If we can articulate the importance, we can address the feeling and take an actionable step on what to do with that item. For example, I did not need to keep all of my dad's sweatshirts. I kept one of Tigger, because he was definitely Tigger to me—my dad was the only one! And I still have a super soft red angora turtleneck that I "borrowed" from him when I was in high school. I love that one so much!

Once you figure out the meaning, ask yourself: What am I looking for from that thing? There's no need to justify it to anyone. Instead, try to articulate the meaning and let yourself know it. That will take you one step closer to deciding what to do with it. Go or stay? Just find out why you want or don't want it. There may be a weighty meaning and power you're giving to the object that may be stifling you in some way.

Letting Go, Keeping the Memory

When I met Sherri years ago, she was in her late 70s, moving out of a home she had lived in with her three kids and her husband. Her husband had passed away quite a few years before, and her kids were out of the house with kids of their own. Sherri was going to move into a senior community to live closer to her boyfriend. It was so sweet that she made a point to tell me they were not moving in together. Instead, they would have separate apartments in the same senior community, which I thought was amazingly adorable.

Sherri had begun downsizing in preparation for the move but called me because she still had difficulty letting go of some things. She was going to miss her beautiful garden that she and her husband designed. Sherri loved gardening and planted all the flowers herself. She loved freshly cut flowers and displayed them in almost every room in her home. Friends and family started giving her vases, and so her collection began. When I came in, Sherri and I started looking at all the vases she hadn't yet donated. We came upon this beautiful cloudy soft pink vase.

We were sitting on her couch, and she held the vase in her hand for a long time.

Finally, she said, "Lisa, I just don't know what to do with this one." She started tearing up. She told me about her best friend, Sally, who had bought it for her many years before. Their kids had grown up together, and they had become inseparable and comforted each other when their husbands passed. Recently, her friend moved across the country to be closer to her kids and grandkids. It was a devastating loss for Sherri as she had no other friends left in the cul-de-sac. Her friend's move had influenced her decision to move as well.

As she held the vase, I gently said, "Did you get out of it what your friend intended for you?"

She thought for a while and said, "I believe so, as she gave it to me with such love, and I cherished it. I remember using it for special occasions, and Sally would bring me flowers from her garden to put in the vase. I treasured it." She paused, gazing at the vase, and then said, "Even though I don't want to bring it to my new home, it'll be okay."

I'll never know why Sherri decided not to bring it with her; maybe the pain of seeing it reminded her of her faraway friend, so it was too difficult for her. Sherri said she wasn't giving up the love from her friend just because she didn't want to take something that she had given to her. "This vase is going to go on. We will donate it, and someone will see it on a shelf and buy it for their friend or themselves, and they'll love it and cherish it just as I did all these years."

A great way to think of recycling is that when we donate and repurpose, we recycle the love that remains in that object.

Sherri isn't the only one with a collection or two. In many clients' homes, an event or even a passing comment gives everyone the idea it's something the person desires—it's funny. For example, someone says they like pigs and, before long, the person has a collection of little pig tchotchkes all over the house. My mom started a frog collection for a friend for her backyard, maybe as a housewarming present. After my mom passed, I went through her "gift closet" and found a few frogs I offered to her friend, trusting Mom intended them for her. We cried because it was so ridiculous, sweet—and true.

When there is a death in the family of someone who played a big part in your life, grieving is challenging, ever-changing, and endless, especially if the love is deep—the stronger the love, the longer and harder the mourning process. People get stuck in a soup of emotions and can't recover. They want to keep everything the way as it was when the person was alive. And that's okay—until it's not okay and hinders their health. All grieving is personal and can take on a life of its own. I have worked with many clients who have gone through a divorce that can feel like a death. The loss is so intense it's difficult to function. In a divorce, there is a death—the death of that relationship. There is the death of the dream, the expected life with that person. And the happy ever after. What it was and what it might have been in the future. We hold onto whatever memories we can recall. That is the subconscious protecting us in this fragile state.

17
Spatulas

Chapter Thirteen

The Stories We Tell Ourselves

There is no passion to be found in playing small—and settling
for a life that is less than the one you are capable of living.
—Nelson Mandela

A conversation with my friend, Cindy Battino, CEO of Transformational Healing, became philosophical. I told her that no matter what you believe in—a higher power, the universe, God, Goddess, Buddha, the powers that be, or nothing—you still believe in something. Suppose you surrender to something far greater than you and trust that the universal intention of a dream will manifest in some way. It may not turn out quite how you thought it would, so it could be something even better or just different than you imagined. It might not look the same as the movie you played in your head over and over again, but I hope that if you keep your eyes and heart open, knowing the intention and feel of it, you will recognize your dream when it comes to life.

When we trust that a bigger picture and overall story is unfolding for our lives, we can surrender and come to a place of peace, freedom, and security. The things we wanted to happen did not because they were not supposed to happen. Even though we hoped and wished and prayed, it's often a "Why ask Why?" kind of thing. There is often no logical reason. Why didn't I get pregnant again? We did everything right. Why did my friend die at 56 years old? There is no real reason that we can logically understand.

There is good news: We can embrace and enjoy our lives. Trust that whatever goes on in our world, whatever has changed from our original vision, can still unfold, even if in a much different form.

———————

When holding onto physical items, roles, or painful events, letting them go does not happen overnight. Instead, the process takes time, begins as a revelation in the mind, and gradually lands in the heart.

My friend, Jonny B, told me about his Auntie Ollie, who lived in a small, modest house. Her daughter ran away from home at 17. Their relationship had always been rocky, but her daughter's sudden absence seemed to break her spirit.

Soon after, she began to indulge in "retail therapy," charging all her purchases on several credit cards. It's been over twenty years, and Auntie Ollie now has a house with one bedroom filled to the ceiling with yarn, fabric, Christmas ribbon, and other crafting supplies, as well as a mountain of debt because of her spending that she now can't afford. It didn't just start, however. She began by telling herself a story.

A story about her daughter and their relationship. A story with an absence of severed ties and hurtful words on both sides that can never be unsaid or forgotten. A story where her daughter never grows up and never runs away from home. A story that Auntie Ollie believes to this day. She cannot let go of this version of her daughter or the story she tells herself. And now, this story has morphed into the excess items clogging up her daughter's old bedroom, filling a void.

Unfortunately, Auntie Ollie concentrated all her energy on the fact that her daughter left—seemingly out of the blue. She conveniently forgot the years and months of fighting and harsh words that led up to the final event of her young daughter taking her future into her own hands and leaving. Perhaps Auntie Ollie clings to this story as a defense mechanism. Maybe she's living in fear, worried for her daughter's safety every waking moment. Or perhaps she believes this story protects her from the reality that her daughter is never coming home.

After writing about Jonny B's Auntie Ollie, I realized that I told myself a story as well—a story that I held onto for thirty years.

———

When I was in my late 20s, I dated a great guy for about two years. He was handsome, smart, athletic, funny, and an incredible dancer. We always had a lot of fun, and he always supported and encouraged me. While our families were opposites—he came from an affluent, educated, wealthy family, and I did not—it never bothered me. When you love someone, you love someone for who they are, not what they have or what their family has. That was my belief. And I thought it was his as well.

A month after our second anniversary, when he asked me to come to his apartment, I arrived full of energy and excited to see him, as usual. Oddly, he had locked the door, so I had to ring the doorbell instead of walking right in. He gave me a half-body hug and then completely ambushed me, saying that our relationship wasn't working for him and he didn't want to stay together. As I stood there stunned, he handed me a box of the things I had kept there. I remember breaking down in a super ugly cry—the slobbering-kid kind of cry—right in front of him, saying I didn't understand. Why? What happened? He gave me no answers and said, "Goodbye." I had to drive myself home, head throbbing and hardly able to see through my tears.

There had been no warning signs that I had noticed. For days I didn't sleep and was completely out of it. Finally, after a couple of weeks of silence, my former boyfriend came over and told me how much he missed and loved me and that the only way we would break up again would be if I broke up with him. We got back together, and that "perfection" lasted a few months. However, I was on edge the whole time, waiting for things to fall apart again.

One day he called and said, "Can you meet me at my apartment today at 3?" My gut knew what was going to happen. At least this time, I decided that I would be in my safe space when it happened. I refused. Instead, I said, "Come to my apartment at 3:30." This time, when he broke my heart for the second and final time, I didn't cry. I wasn't upset.

In fact, I felt nothing except betrayal, naïveté, anger, and a desperate need for it all to be over so I could move on.

As he walked out, he stopped, turned back, and said, "You know the thing about your family having no money always bothered me." Then he turned again and walked out the door. That comment crushed me. More than breaking my heart, his words made me feel ashamed, embarrassed, and angry at my past, my family, and how I grew up.

For thirty years, I held on to that feeling of embarrassment and shame and never told anyone his last words to me. Ironically, I didn't want anyone to think badly of *him*. More so, that wounded part of me wondered if others would also leave me if they knew I came from a blue-collar family.

The pain of those vicious, parting words stung deep. So deep that when I thought about our relationship years later, I only focused on how mean he was to me in those last moments and wondered what I did to deserve that. Only after doing my inner work did I realize that if I were going to hold onto that resentment until the day I died, I would be unable to acknowledge all the good times we shared. The long-term relationship part just wasn't meant to be. I'll never know what drove him to say those horrible words to me. At this point, it is not for me to know or judge.

Today, I no longer look back on our relationship as a mistake, just another lesson I had to learn to bring me exactly where I need to be. However, it took roughly thirty years and countless hours of therapy before I could change the story I believed about myself and how others perceived me.

Telling ourselves these stories serves a purpose, like keeping us safe for a little while. But like most coping mechanisms, they take over our lives and often become obstacles to seeing the bigger, more expansive, beautiful picture. And if we keep telling ourselves the same story, we miss out on all the other ones we could create.

There is good news: We are the authors of our stories. So we can choose to reread the same story or end it and start the sequel. We decide how the next chapter begins because we have the power.

17
Spatulas

Part II

INTENTIONAL

This step can be emotional because some items have baggage.
You examine any guilt or reasons behind
why you've kept these things.

Chapter Fourteen

What He Couldn't See

Vince and I started working on his townhouse five days after our walk-through and continued working together for six to eight hours each week for eight months. He worked so hard, mentally and physically. He patiently explained and was passionate about computer terminology and online trading as I mentored and walked him through The LITL System.

"Vince, what subjects are you not interested in?"

"Organizing!"

Touché.

We worked together for at least 190 hours, and in that time, we managed to donate over 3,000 books from every genre imaginable. I could not even wrap my head around trying to understand some titles. A few times, my van would sag in the back because of the weight of books.

Wednesday and Friday were our usual working days. Mondays and Thursdays were his garbage and recycling pickup days.

Vince's trash cans would be overflowing, and there was always more. I stuffed the bags full, and they were often too overwhelming for Vince to bring out to the curb for Monday morning pickups.

At the end of a session, I would tell him, "Don't worry, our pickup is tomorrow, and I have room in the van, so I'll take some to load in my trash can, and then we'll be back around 7 to get the rest out." Since there was often more than I could take, my husband, daughter, and I would arrive on Sunday evenings to put out more of the recycling and trash from the homework he accomplished between our sessions, ready for Monday mornings.

He knew the homework was optional, and he appreciated that. "I didn't get much done this weekend. But I finally went through my box of pictures. I found three envelopes full from a trip to Canada with my younger brother before I went to the US Naval Academy in Annapolis. I had forgotten all about it. Now that was a good time!" He winked. "And look at these! I looked pretty good in my Dress Blues."

A younger, happier Vince smiled back at me from the photo. I was pleased that I was beginning to see hints of that happier and more relaxed man during our work together, and I anticipated seeing more of him soon. He was very proud of having served his country and making a difference.

"After my first knee surgery, I had to step down, Medically Retired. Even though a military career was all I ever dreamed about, if I had stayed, none of this—" gesturing around his home, "—would have happened." He paused reflectively. "Looking back, I didn't take advantage of the confidence I had when I was younger. I had fun, but I wish I had taken even more risks and spoken up for what I wanted and believed. Now it's too late." His face fell again as he pondered a future where he no longer made a difference. But all that was going to change.

Working closely with Vince, I kept learning more about this wicked smart man, including that for years he had been living with depression, anxiety, and Asperger Syndrome. While steadily sorting through the physical evidence of his past, Vince was opening up more and more emotionally. With each box, he felt more confidence and courage in finally facing his past—healing and finding peace. "I can't believe I surrounded and cocooned myself so unkindly for so long, but through decluttering with you and working with my therapist, I realize that trying to protect myself with stuff couldn't keep out the hurt, betrayal, pain, and horrible flashbacks. Literally going through it, mentally and physically, is the only way out."

I nodded. "You're right! Grow through what you go through."

"Oh, I like that." He grinned.

While sitting one day on a break, I asked him, "Why did you hire me, Vince?"

"Well, as you know, I did a lot of research, and each person I talked to before you asked how much stuff I had, if there was room to move around, and how quickly I wanted it out. I knew I needed to get the stuff out of my townhouse, but I needed the mental tools and decision-making processes in place. I could tell they just wanted a quick turnover. I knew I needed more. Then, I called you, and you asked me first how I felt in my space and what prompted me to reach out for help. You asked me about me, and my hobbies, what I like to do, what I did for a living, and how I spend my day! You didn't try to sell me on the quickest and easiest way to get rid of my stuff. Remember that first call?"

I smiled. "Like it was yesterday."

He continued. "You told me what to expect and reassured me that we would go as quickly or as slowly as I liked. You were there for me."

"I remember telling you about The LITL System and how easy it would be. Haha! Simple, not easy."

"Yes! And you even joked that you didn't care what my house looked like when you got here; what you really cared about was how I felt when you left! I was glad to have the option to meet you first, but I felt relieved even before we met because I knew I had found my person, you, the one who could help me. Thank you!"

When we had finished the basement level, the first-floor den, the eating area, and the kitchen, I wanted to surprise him in some way, and also, we needed to change the energy in the townhouse. So, I arranged for a professional cleaning company to deep clean the space for him while I took him out to brunch (definitely an occasion for him!). They vacuumed and dusted, clearing out years and years of old energy and built-up muck.

When we returned from brunch and walked into his home, we both took the deepest, cleanest breath of fresh air in and out.

"Surprise, Vince! You are amazing."

Looking every which way, trying to take it all in, he was speechless for minutes. "This place looks and feels completely different. Wow, how did you do this? Why did you do this?" Hugs and tears flowed, and lots of wandering around and touching everything like he hadn't lived there before.

"It's a brand-new start for you, Vince. You have worked so hard. I want you to see your accomplishments."

The kitchen looked brand new. And finally, we could actually walk in and sit in the den. He said excitedly, "Now I can start watching TV and reading here." The cleaners had opened the drapes and cleaned the bay windows; light sprang from every corner. The formerly dank, dreary, life-sucking space felt like a completely different room.

As he walked around, I saw it. There it was, the sparkle in his eye of the confident man in his military pictures. But he was still hesitant. His confident self, who had not been out in a long time, was still cautious and a little scared, though he was almost there.

That day we looked at the before pictures—the ones he did not want me to take—neither of us could believe it was the same space.

Shaking his head, eyes wide and a little glossy, he marveled. "I just didn't see the clutter. I just didn't see what I was actually living in, and I still can't believe I lived like that for so long. I just didn't see it. But I guess I needed it for a time. Make sure you put me in your book when you write it."

17
Spatulas

Chapter Fifteen

Fear and Procrastination

Clutter is not just physical stuff. It's old ideas, toxic relationships and bad habits. Clutter is anything that does not support your better self.
—Eleanor Brownn

Have you ever opened a random drawer? You find an old pile of papers and think: "I have no idea why I kept these papers!" Or your grade school bin that you open up decades later, and the names on all the little notes you and your friends passed each other are a distant memory. It's true—we don't always know why we hold onto things until we ask intentional questions and hear our excuses.

"How long has it been there, and when was the last time I needed or used it?" "Does it serve a purpose?" "Do I love it or just want to keep it?"

We all put off looking through our stuff.

"Why take the time even to decide if we should go through it?"

"It's not hurting anything, so why even think about it?"

"There's no reason to. It's not getting in the way."

Only when a significant life event occurs—a move, a death in the family, or some catastrophic event—that forces us to ask ourselves the tough questions is when the overwhelm hits us. How do you begin to wade through decades of items, memories, and subsequent emotions?

First, you choose to start. Block out a date and time window with yourself and your family so you actually do it. It's like any other important appointment in your life; you have to schedule it to get it done. You may need to mentally prepare to answer questions about some items you uncover.

When I go back and look at my stuff (and yes, I, too, have bins of memories that I have saved through the years), if I don't remember who gave it to me or have forgotten the memory specifically attached to an item, I will donate it. Someone else could always use what I no longer want or need. If it's papers or flyers that don't have a date or don't have a significant recollection for me, I put them into recycling if I can or throw them away.

If you are going through things and you have to ask yourself, "What the heck is this? Where did it even come from?" the answer is quite clear—no need for further discussion.

There is also a significant amount of fear associated with the thought of going through things and revisiting unpleasant events. We may have stashed things so far back in our closets, attics, basements, and memories because we did not want to see them again. But the FEAR (False Evidence Appearing Real) that my clients go through is worse than actually opening up the box and going through the contents. I recommend taking a break if it becomes too much, staying hydrated throughout the process, and, if it becomes too much to handle alone, reaching out for help.

How about the secrets we keep from ourselves? If we don't see it, it doesn't exist. We don't have to deal with it if we're unaware. Many people only want to remember the good stuff in their lives, so they get rid of every other item linked to a negative memory, which is fine as long as we are intentional about why we are throwing it away. And at least take a look and see what is in the box, cabinet, or space to ensure we don't miss anything. We cannot explore or begin to heal what we won't even allow ourselves to acknowledge.

My job is not to tell people what to get rid of or what to keep. I am merely a soundboard in a brainstorming session to establish what's really important in their lives. Watching them and "listening" to their honest, personal struggles and secret fears helps me create the best space to be in and hold for them. I trust that I will find the right words to ask the key questions that will move them along to achieve their goal.

After working with clients with deep personal issues for almost two decades, I've learned to listen to what they're not saying and how better to help them move on. Most times, we realize the goal isn't just cleaning out the bedroom or the basement; it is to heal their soul and help them feel free again so they can enjoy their lives and not remain captive to the past.

17
Spatulas

Chapter Sixteen

Self-Care...in an odd sort of way

Would've, Could've, Should've—The Holy Trinity of Regret
—Gary Gulman, comedian

Sometimes, I just want to feel sorry for myself. That's what I call "sitting in your dirty diapers." I sit in the middle of my mess of a situation and pout and complain and feel sorry for myself. I throw myself a pity party, but it's not fun, and I'm usually all alone. And guess what? There's nothing wrong with it. It serves a purpose for a little while—relieving some of the stress, and just getting it all out in the open. Kind of like journaling, just doing a brain dump of everything I'm feeling. And after I'm done, in some weird way, I am comforted and usually laugh a little bit. It may feel indulgent, pointless, and even gross afterward, but my brain and body got something out of it. I usually feel lighter and ready to go. Trust me when I tell you within the two years of writing this book, I have sat in my dirty diapers more than a few times.

A group of my girlfriends and I have another unique way to "cope" and get things off our chests. We've dubbed it "Five minutes to bitch." We don't need answers or want anyone to feel sorry for us or find a solution. We don't want to discuss our unsettledness. We just need five minutes to get whatever is bothering us out of our heads.

"Five minutes" is a healthier, more constructive option than sitting in dirty diapers. Sometimes life is difficult, it stinks, and we need to give ourselves a chance to complain about it and even feel sorry for ourselves in our current situation. Life isn't good if you stay in pain and can't remove it somehow. We lose track of time when we hold onto pain, feel sorry for ourselves, or blame others for our problems for way too long. Life slips by. The key to the "five minutes" tool, or whatever is healthy to disrupt your agitated state of being, is to get all the negative feelings, thoughts, and energy out. Acknowledge them, confront them, and take action to change—your diapers, your space, your circumstances, and most importantly, your mindset. We cannot explore or begin to heal what we won't even allow ourselves to acknowledge. Taking action changes thinking instead of thinking of changing your actions. Only then can we heal and move on.

———————

It's a cliche, but it's true: I am my own worst critic. I'm so hard on myself. My internal voice is there in that board meeting in my head, where I play all the roles. It's continuously happening, with or without me, making me doubt and second-guess myself.

> I should've said this and not that. Ugh, why do I do that?
> I definitely shouldn't have eaten that! I should've stuck to my diet!
> I could've done it if I had known earlier, but now, it's too late.
> I could've gone, but no one invited me.
> I would've taken out the trash if I wasn't so tired.
> I would've been able to organize if I had help and the right storage bins.

We get stuck in the negative cycle and keep "shoulding" on ourselves. Have you ever done that? Most of us beat ourselves up with secret regrets and personal doubts. Especially if something doesn't go our way, the outcome wasn't what we expected, or we're embarrassed or scared of making the "wrong" decision.

How about the secrets you keep from yourself? These are the things we don't want to admit to ourselves. "I'll just eat one cookie—that won't ruin my cleanse," Or "I need this yellow shirt. It's a completely different shade than my four other yellow shirts!" Or "I'll have vodka instead of wine. It doesn't have any sugar!" We will never move forward or stop shoulding on ourselves if we are unwilling to acknowledge what's really going on.

So how do we stop the endless barrage of the "Should've, could've, would've"?

I mention throughout the book that the first step is to be aware and to embrace our fear of letting go mentally and physically because, once the words are out of our mouth, once we've eaten the first spoonful right out of the ice cream container—it's done. We can't go back in time and change things, but we can stop the behavior. If we practice becoming aware of when we get caught up in this cycle, we can make a decision right then to break the habit. If you are past the point of no return but realize it, make an intentional decision to work on catching yourself in the future.

Of course, it's easier said than done. Unfortunately, the negative self-talk, the critical tapes that play in our heads, cannot be erased or thrown out. We must learn to play a new tape with affirming words louder than critical ones. It will take time and may require the professional help of a therapist or coach. It is possible. I've done it and seen the positive results in myself and others. Like any significant change you want to make, it takes commitment and consistency.

And that's part of being human—learning from our mistakes and hopefully learning enough from them to start making positive choices. We are all a work in progress—so be kind to yourself and accept that a good goal today is to do better than we did yesterday.

Chapter Seventeen

Keep it in the Family

One holiday, years before I was a professional organizer, my three brothers, our parents, and I started talking about some of the furniture and artwork in our parents' home. For example, we had a beautiful oak dining table reconstructed into a large pedestal table in the living room.

"Mom and I went to a vintage store in Chicago to buy this table, so I'd really like to have it," I said to my brothers.

Paul looked at me with his silly grin. "Well, I really like it too. Maybe I want it."

That started a great discussion on who wanted certain things in their house. So, we decided to walk around the house and discuss some of the bigger things and who wanted what, like the double-wide rocking chair that fit all four of us as kids. We all had different and wonderful memories of the same piece. My youngest brother, Vic, wanted it because he had little kids then, and his memory was by far the funniest. He remembered loving playing Dracula; he had the cape and everything, and the rocker was his coffin that he rose out of and said to scare us, "I've come to sauuk your blood."

Then there was this old door that my dad stripped down, replaced the eight windows with mirrors, and created this fantastic piece that he placed at the end of our hallway. When one of my brothers tried to claim it, I said, "No way, I get it. I was with Dad when he garbage-picked it off the street while I scrunched down in the front seat of our station wagon!"

I'll always remember that wonderful evening with my brothers and parents. It was such a fun, cathartic, emotional journey back down memory lane. The time we spent together talking about things and all the different memories we each had about the same item was so sweet.

I encourage my clients to be intentional when they go through their things because memories may be associated with particular items that adult children or relatives will want to share with them. Talk to your family. Instead of just giving them items now or leaving them for after you pass away, ask which pieces they would like. In addition, I suggest that my clients write little notes on things they want to give to their kids or to keep for themselves. I remember Mom telling me, "Oh, you'll remember," and I'd say, "Nope, probably not, and even if I do, it would be really great if we had a handwritten note from you with just a few lines about the story behind it. Also, having your writing will be such a wonderful gift."

After my mom passed, my daughter and nieces received items she had put aside for them, and when we saw her writing, it was like hearing my mom speak again—a little piece of heaven.

If you're avoiding having this difficult conversation with your loved ones because you think it's morbid, you're right! But we all die, so we have to do it, and in the long run, taking care of these details ahead of time allows your family time to grieve after you die without worrying about who gets what or, more importantly, your wishes. You also have peace of mind that the family heirlooms will still have a home; even if they donate them, they'll know the significance of items for you.

Instead of procrastinating further because "I don't want to take the time to do it. My family gets everything anyway, so they'll have to deal with it when I die," take the time and make some more memories with your family. For example, discuss the stories behind the wedding china from your Aunt Helen and the porcelain chamber pot from your great-grandfather's travels! We keep certain items because of their connection to loved ones who have already passed. And that is a great reason to keep a few special things—but not fill the house with them.

And yes, sometimes it is too emotional for everyone to discuss everything together. However, it's often more emotional in a different way for one person to go through all your belongings while they're grieving for you, dealing with other stresses in their life, and having to make big decisions without you.

17
Spatulas

Chapter Eighteen

Courage Accompanies Fear

Any place in your life you complain about is linked
to not taking personal responsibility.
—Elie Wiesel, *Night, Dawn, Day*

One of the most challenging type of client we work with has a victim mentality. Often, a family member calls me when they can't take it anymore. They are at the end of their rope. I show up, and the potential client doesn't want anything to do with me. They are "perfectly content" to remain surrounded by piles of toys, books, clothes, and what have you because they're "fine, everything's fine, nothing needs to be done."

Even though the family has offered time and again to help, "the victim" has pushed away anyone willing to help and is convinced they have nowhere to turn. "No one helps me. No one loves me or cares about me. I can't change—this is who I am. Why can't you just let me be? I could if I wanted to, but it is too overwhelming. I don't know where to start. And no one will notice anyway, so why even try?"

Some of my clients who fall into this category end up working with me after I explain The LITL System. Remember, my job is not to throw everything out. My job is to lessen the stress of their surroundings, and help them gain confidence in knowing what's important rather than blaming their situation on outside sources or reasons.

I often consult my therapist or life coach colleagues to ensure I'm guiding my clients in the right direction.

"We create and live our worst nightmares due to fear. That part of our psyche is convinced that the fear is real. We will unconsciously sabotage our life to prove that those fears are accurate," Cindy Battino told me over coffee. "So, when things happen, that young part of us can say, 'I told you so; I knew bad things were going to happen. I was right.'"

"Wow," I said, nodding. "That makes so much sense. So many of my clients get stuck there!"

I wanted to delve into this inner dynamic more, hoping it would better help me serve this type of client. When I contacted another therapist friend, Craig James, Co-Founder of Insight into Action Therapy, he shared:

> "We are where we are because it feeds us in some way. It serves us. A part of our psyche gets off on being stuck, being the victim. It truly feeds us. Humans do not do anything unless there is a reward, a payoff. We get something out of it. Now, this doesn't mean being selfish, of course. Many people do things because it makes them feel good, which is also a reward."

Our primal brain wants us to stay where it perceives we are safe. To go outside that zone is to put ourselves in danger, or so we assume. Staying where it is safe means we don't have to think about it—we don't have to make changes or work on anything.

So, this cycle continues as long as the person feels secure in what they believe is safe. Meanwhile, most of us tend to remain in our comfort zone. Stretching out of it can be painful and scary. But, if we stay there, drowning in our fear and victimhood, we will miss out on the joy that comes after growing through the pain.

I keep reiterating throughout the book, and Cindy recently reminded me that a person in victim mode must first recognize that they're in victim mode. Then, once they know they are stuck in a victim mentality and want to change, the next step is to become intentional about the language they're using.

However, the key here is that they must be the agents of their change. No one else—not loved ones, not therapists—can make that change for them.

If they have been saying things to themselves and others such as "poor me," "why me," "this always happens to me," or "I'll never find someone who will love me," they need to change the narrative, rewrite the script of their movie. If they've complained about not liking an aspect of their life—work, home, relationships—but have never done anything about it, just taking responsibility for the negative thought is a first step toward changing the old patterns.

I have stayed in my comfort zone because of fear and probably missed out on beautiful opportunities. And I often wish I could go back to being less aware of myself and staying safe because growth is often painful, yet while the unknown is scary—it can also be exciting.

So, I get it. Making changes can take a while, is challenging, and often emotionally draining. To look inward and see where we are holding ourselves back takes courage. It's much easier to blame someone or something else rather than commit, do the work, and ultimately find joy.

Remember, we all have the power. We can choose: change, step out of our comfort zone, and get the help we need, or remain a prisoner of our fear. It is not easy, but it is simple.

17
Spatulas

Chapter Nineteen

Dreaming New Dreams

You are never too old to set another goal or to dream a new dream.
—Les Brown

Carole was a high-powered lawyer on Capitol Hill. Yet, even with her insane work hours, she still found time to indulge her passion for genealogy. In addition, her mother often visited from New Jersey, and they spent hours making beautiful necklaces with the precious stones they purchased. It was how Carole relaxed from her stressful job.

When I arrived at the cozy bungalow with her sister Gina, Carole was still in the hospital recovering from a setback with her MS. Gina refused to go in with me. She held a hand up to her nose. "My sister has lived here almost twenty years, along with three cats and a dog. It's filled from top to bottom. Prepare yourself." She wrinkled up her face. "The smell is intense."

I grinned. "No worries! I always bring my allergy meds with me as well as face masks. And trust me, I've been in some pretty interesting houses." As soon as I opened the door, the reek of cat urine and dog feces assaulted me. The smell was worse than I expected. The house had been closed for a month while Carole was in the hospital. I put on my mask and walked ahead on my own into what was once a cute foyer.

"I've had the animals with me." Gina raised her voice a little to reach me from the front porch.

The house had obviously been built in the 1940s and I could still see a glimpse of its charm under the piles and stacks surrounding me. "What are all these books here?" I called back to Gina.

She peeked in with her hand still over her nose. "Carole was researching our family tree and loved history and genealogy." She waved at me. "Do you have an extra mask?"

I handed her one, and we stepped further into the house so she could give me a tour.

"Take a look in this room. It's a whole bedroom dedicated to our lineage." She shook her brown, highlighted hair. "Stan, her ex, was a real piece of work. Do you know, he just up and left when she was first diagnosed? Said he didn't sign up to be a nurse. They had been trying for a few years to get pregnant. Completely cleaned out their joint bank account. Can you believe that? The divorce shattered something in her." She went to take a deep breath, then coughed. "And then right after that, mom died. It was all just too much."

As we walked through the rest of the house, Gina showed me another bedroom dedicated to "all things crafts," where Carole would make jewelry, paint, and whatever other crafts caught her fancy. Because boxes of beads, wires, fabrics, paint pots, and jewelry-making tools filled the room, we couldn't walk in more than two steps at first. Gina stood at the doorway with me and explained. "But jewelry is her real passion aside from genealogy. After our mother passed away, Carole just stopped making jewelry and doing her crafts and all the things she loved. As you can see, though, she kept making purchases of items and things she wanted to use in the future."

Gina continued. "Carole and our mother had sold some of their jewelry at craft shows here and there and dreamed of making a big business out of it." But instead, Carole's dreams were stacked around her tiny home.

After Carole stabilized and came home from the hospital, I worked with her for several months.

After we uncovered yet another box full of unopened beads and wire, Carole stopped and said, "You know, I told myself I was keeping my mother close and holding on to her by buying all this to keep our dream alive." She paused and smiled ruefully. "Making jewelry is still therapeutic for me. However, now I realize I don't need quite so much stuff. I'll never get through it all on my own."

I was impressed with how quickly we were making progress, and I asked her how she could let go of decades worth of stuff in such a short time and make hard decisions.

She said, "Lisa, after being in and out of the hospital so much, I would lay there in yet another hospital bed, too tired to watch TV or read, so all I did was think. And I thought, this time I'm going to die, and I cannot leave all this mess to my family. They shouldn't have to weed through all my hurt and pain. All this stuff is an outcome of all the crap I went through in such a short time. I am smart, yet I couldn't grasp why every little thing was so important for me to keep. So I insulated and isolated myself, not letting anyone in or anything out because I couldn't bear the pain of losing another person I cared about."

After we finished working together, Carole's dream changed from having a business with her mom to using jewelry as therapy. That way, she could still keep her mother's memory alive while keeping her house comfortable and organized.

Letting go of a dream is difficult and often painful, as is any change. The great thing about working with a professional organizer who gets it and isn't just about "getting rid of" your stuff and creating a picture-perfect space is that you don't need to go through this process in isolation. Watching Carole grow as a person and take bold new steps into the future was a joy to witness.

Bill was another client who surprised me by masterfully changing his story.

Writing was Bill's passion, practically from the moment he could hold a pencil. And like most writers, he dreamed of being a prize-winning author someday. His library reminded me a little of Vince's library—it was vast and filled with books across multiple genres. While he had read most of them, others were for "someday."

"And the rest," laughed Bill, "I bought because they seemed necessary for an aspiring Pulitzer Prize winner!"

He took several courses to study the art of writing to help him become a stronger author. Together, we sat at the maple dining room table and sifted through piles of notes, manuals, and workbooks from all those courses.

"So, is that what you do? You're an author?" I asked.

He shook his head, his smile a little bitter. "See all these photos?"

I glanced toward the stairwell, where frames of smiling adults and children lovingly covered the wall.

"Married my college sweetheart. Had a few too many kids." He laughed and shook his head, his face filled with love. "Wouldn't change any of that for the world. However, it meant I had to give up that Pulitzer dream. Couldn't provide a good life for my girls and boys trying to become the next Hemingway!" He sighed and turned back to the papers. "Did try writing in my spare time, but somewhere along the way, I just—lost the passion, I guess."

Bill took his responsibilities very seriously, and even though he wasn't thrilled with his profession, he didn't hate it and stayed at the same full-time job for years. He paid the bills and kept his family fed, safe, and under one roof for 45 years.

When I met him, all the kids had moved out and had kids of their own. "It looks like you have a lot of grandkids to spoil!" I said, pointing to all the photos.

He half-smiled and shook his head. "Don't get to see them nearly as often as we'd like. But Carolyn and I try to visit them when they are out of school. It's a long way to go for just a weekend." He cleared his throat. "Ah, but that's okay. They have lives of their own now."

Bill's routine was the same for every session I had with him. We would meet in his kitchen, chat with Carolyn before she went to work, get a cup of coffee, and head to the library. He would share his memories with me, and eventually, we would begin sorting through books and papers that were already pretty well categorized. For the books, he would decide if he wanted to donate to the local library or the college nearby, where he had friends. You might wonder what help he needed if he had already organized things. He needed support, understanding, and someone to talk things through with him. He was very organized but couldn't seem to focus as much and didn't want to be alone and have to make all the decisions. I became a pseudo-daughter who had the time and experience to help. And I miss my dad every day, so we both enjoyed our time together.

One day, we came across a big file folder filled with legal pads full of his old writings. "This folder looks important, Bill. Take a look," I said, handing it to him.

In a flash, excitement, regret, love, and a hint of anger moved across his expressive face. Then, as he began to flip through the folder, he said, "This brings back so many wonderful, exciting, and, of course, sad memories from my past."

We took a moment, he refilled our coffees, and then we sat down to talk about what was coming up for him.

After a short time, he said, "You know what, this will be my homework for the next week, and probably more. I'm going to take a look at what I have in here and see if I can resurrect any of it." He put the folder aside, and we finished our goal for the day's session.

When I returned the following week, he had all his stories laid out on his dining room table. I was so happy for him and impressed by how he organized everything.

Laughing, he said, "Most of it is garbage and amateur. I can't believe I was such a horrible writer and had aspirations of being famous!" He saved two legal pads containing a story he started writing about his childhood to continue seeing what came out. "Even if it's not that good," he shrugged, "at least my grandkids will know who I was and how I grew up."

Here is a 75-year-old man with nothing but time to do as he pleases, and he chose to go back and follow that dream and reinvent himself as a writer, even if it was just for him and his grandkids. Bill's passion and commitment blew me away. Sometimes, the dreams and goals we once thought we lost turn out way differently than we expected. I'm so glad Bill found the right path for him.

––––––––––

Kari was a client I helped out with after COVID. She told me about a painting in her childhood home that was the only possession she wanted to keep after her mother passed. "It was just a painting," she said. "It wasn't worth any money, and I wouldn't have sold it even if it had been worth something." She just had great memories of it. Smiling, she said, "I remember sitting drinking hot cocoa with my mom, and that painting hung on the wall right behind her head. The simple landscape and colors were calming, and it will always remind me of those special mother-daughter talks and private time I had alone with my mom."

Unfortunately, when helpers cleared out the house after her mother passed away, Kari hadn't shared her desire to keep the painting, so they donated it with many other items.

"I was devastated and felt really bad for a long time. I felt like a part of me had been ripped away because I had anticipated having the painting in my home where I could reminisce about the wonderful times with my mom."

Here's the good news: A few years later, Kari and her husband were in an art gallery, just browsing and enjoying their afternoon together, when she turned a corner, and a beautiful painting immediately drew her attention.

This painting wasn't the one from her childhood memory, but looking at it, the same feelings from all those years ago completely overwhelmed her. "It's like this painting instantly transported me back to my childhood and it reminded me of all those beautiful moments of peace and serenity I had with my mom." Kari purchased the painting, and it now hangs in her home.

Yes, she lost the dream of having her mother's painting in her own home, but she found something that reminds her of her mom when she looks at it. It's a new painting representing an old dream.

If only. Those must be the two saddest words in the world.
—Mercedes Lackey

When I was younger, my dream was to be a Broadway star.

My family was a theater family. When I was still quite young, I began taking dance lessons, and later on, my brothers and I would dance and sing at many local community events. When they were older, my brothers, Drew and Paul, toured the world in various shows and danced on Broadway. I was sure I would follow them one day. I attended the High School of Performing Arts in Chicago—like the school in *Fame*.

My dream was to make it big. I spent countless hours in dance studios, took vocal lessons, and performed in as many musicals and plays as I could. I toured the United States and Canada as the Count in Sesame Street Live and had a blast!

While I was on tour, someone stabbed one of my best friends to death on the street in Chicago. I met Danny when we were 16 in our sophomore year at the Performing Arts High School. Fortunately, the dance captain gave me a leave from the tour to return to Chicago for a few days for the funeral, reuniting with old friends I hadn't seen for five years since graduation.

All too soon, I was back on the road to continue the tour. I remember sitting backstage in my costume, waiting to go on and just crying. Luckily, dressed as the character, I had a full helmet and "head" on my head—no one saw or heard me cry. I felt so alone, with no one to share my grief with and no time to grieve.

I dragged myself back to my one-bedroom apartment when the tour ended and looked around blankly. The thought annihilated me—Danny would not be knocking on the door, a bottle of wine in hand, just ready to hang out. Underneath my grief and shock, I thought, "What am I doing with my life?" I thought about how precious and short life is—that tomorrow is never guaranteed. Was I even enjoying my life? Or was I only going through the motions? Was this really my dream or just all that I ever knew?

Two years later, at age 25, I realized I wasn't enjoying a career in theater. At that point, I had done a few more musicals and Shakespeare in the Park, but I was mostly waitressing to pay my bills. The entertainment business is rough, and I lost my passion for it. I loved performing and dancing, but the constant unknowns and rejections finally got to me. The devastation I felt after every failed audition overwhelmed me. I didn't make this decision lightly. Leaving the theatre after sixteen years was no easy feat, considering the commitment to practice, thousands of auditions, hard work for my body, and mental energy expended. The thought of how much money my parents and I spent on dance classes and performance education haunted me.

After I decided to quit and leave behind my life in the theater, I remember holding onto my dance shoes and some special outfits for a long time. To this day, I have my first (and only) pointe shoes and a few costume pieces. My daughter and I have used them for costumes for Halloween, and they still remind me of my wonderful life.

When I look back at my time as a performer, I am amazed at how much I accomplished, learned, and experienced. I loved so much of it. I danced, met famous people, and made friends I still keep in touch with today. I admit, I still feel a slight twinge of "what if," especially when I see a great musical. However, I made an intentional decision, and in my heart, I know it was the right one.

It is never too late to be what you might have been.
—George Eliot

For Sebastian, a client of one of my therapist partners, Dianne Andruzzi, LCSW, it became a full-blown obsession.

"Sebastian, age 65, is not in denial," she told me. "He knows he is just moving papers from one place to another. But Sebastian dreams of creating the perfect replica of the Battle of Bull Run in his basement, with all the hills and valleys, scattered farmhouses, and both encampments. He is trying to recapture the joy and excitement he felt after he built his first battlefield diorama for a school project. In his mind, all the tiny soldiers and horses, even the paints he's collected, are not just for this model battlefield; he's creating a legacy."

Dianne continued, "His legacy includes the field, the tents, the little model buildings, and boxes and boxes of articles, papers, and information. The sheer number of notes on lighting as well as possible moves that the soldiers could have made in the battle is inconceivable and incredibly detailed."

I asked her, "Who is the intended recipient of his legacy?"

She explained. "Sebastian and his wife have no children. No one to inherit what amounts to an extensive art piece. The project has taken over the entire full, unfinished basement. He idealizes the past to relive the glory days and his pride in the first battlefield replica he designed. He wants something tangible to leave behind, a monument that says, 'my life was worth something!' Something more than the unfulfilling job he's worked his whole adult life to pay the bills. Studying history and building this diorama is a hobby he remains passionate about for almost five decades."

I want to know more about his passion.

She continued. "Sebastian has a PhD, plus two more degrees. But he desires to make an impact through this obsession. He's often told me that he could create something so cutting-edge that it will change the world and he will leave such a mark on the industry. People who see this replica will be emotionally changed by viewing it, and they'll even learn about the actual effects of the weather. He pointed out that you can see the dirt on the hands of the figurines and a homemade sling, for example. The details of the story he shows reveal the humanity of the individual soldiers. He emphasizes that it's not about him. It's about making history come alive! For Sebastian, completing this project is how he will live on after his life ends. He has something to leave to the world. However, it will likely never see the light of day until after he has passed, if at all."

Dianne shared with me the possible outcome. "It's an amazing idea, but Sebastian takes it to the extreme. He cannot make a single move out of fear it will be imperfect and not fully bring this battle to life in a way that adequately honors the true story. What an incredible gift this might be for historians and how sad that such attention to detail and the love he puts into it may never go beyond his basement."

When we were young, we all had dreams—how the movie of our life would turn out. We've played it in our head a thousand times; who we would marry, the kind of career we'd like, dreams of traveling to different places and doing great things. Sometimes we can make these dreams a reality, but often life, health, or other events outside our control intervene, and those old dreams are no longer attainable.

When that happens, it's tempting to stay in the past and hold on to those old dreams and "what ifs." What if I had only bought that house? What if I had accomplished that fitness goal? What if I had more money? More time?

I have worked with clients who cannot let go of the details of an unrealized dream. They feel the train has left the station, so they don't deserve to dream again. Sometimes they're afraid the reality won't live up to the image they created, and then the dream becomes a fantasy they hold onto rather than an attainable goal.

For example, *The Alchemist: A Graphic Novel* by Paulo Coelho is one of my favorite books ever. Every time I read it, I "hear" something different because every time I read it, I am in another place in the journey of my life and need to "hear" something else. In the book, the owner of the china shop located on the way to Mecca has a goal. He has had this goal for many years of getting to Mecca. He knows in his heart he will never get to Mecca, and yet the thought of Mecca, the dream of Mecca, keeps him alive. It's easier for him to hold on to what the holy land represents than to his desire to make his way there. He remains imprisoned in the china shop to avoid the disappointment he anticipates he would experience in Mecca.

———

Dreams are necessary—they give meaning, purpose, and color to our lives. However, while some push us to the next level or goal, other dreams are just there to comfort us. And some are never meant to be. Letting go of old dreams, including associated items, can open up passion for new goals.

What if you had to give up the dream of living by the ocean? Can you get a candle with the ocean scent or design your home with the feel you wanted from living near the water? Create the ambiance that you desire. My mom loved lilacs, and I wanted to be reminded of her and smell lilacs every spring and summer, so I planted two right next to my front door. When I walk out there, I take in the beautiful fragrance, think of my childhood home, and sometimes talk to her. Cutting them and having fresh lilac blossoms inside my home is also wonderful.

The beauty of our dreams is that we are the directors, actors, and writers, so we can always change the script. This power frees us to create a new movie and become intentional about the exciting direction our lives can take—so many possibilities.

17
Spatulas

Chapter Twenty

Escape

Addiction is a distraction from life.
—Cyndi Turner, *Practicing Alcohol Moderation:*
A Comprehensive Workbook

One of my organizers worked with Francie, a middle-aged single woman with personal, medical, and financial struggles. She immersed herself in creativity as a way to escape from her troubles. Many of us do this to relax and "get away." The problem is that Francie shopped every weekend, coming home with bags and bags of crafting products for her potential future projects. By the time we worked with her, her craft room had become so cluttered with supplies that it was no longer a functional space, and it spilled into other rooms and took over one entire floor of her townhouse.

What used to be a creative outlet became another source of stress and worry; still, she continued shopping. She could no longer escape her troubles by crafting and creating projects she loved. The shopping obsession took over. Francie felt trapped and stuck, which is why she called me. My Team Mentor began working with Francie biweekly, and, over the two months, a pattern emerged. First, they would make some progress, create a few open spots, and Francie could part with some of the older items. She allowed the Team Mentor to throw out faded artificial flowers, spools of dry-rotted ribbon and cracked and dried-out paints—over twenty years old and unusable. However, when the Team

Mentor returned, the newly-opened space had new items. When they talked about it, Francie would shake her head and say, "I know I don't need more, but those were on sale, and they're just so cute." Or "Oh, no, I've had those for a while. I just found the bag and moved it up here."

Francie didn't recognize she had a problem. Soon, she flatly refused to part with anything else and in addition, she kept bringing in more stuff every week and hid it in different parts of the house. When we work with a client, we want them to trust us, and it was apparent that Francie was having a difficult time. Finally, after separating her crafts by category and making her craft room more accessible with what was in there, Francie realized she needed more help than just organizing and making her space pretty. She sought help from a therapist, and I hope she got the help she needed with her shopping addiction.

When someone has an addiction, nothing matters except chasing that high. Nothing is more important than feeding that hunger with drugs, alcohol, shopping, or food—whatever their way of numbing the pain happens to be. They cease to see reality as it is. They aren't aware of the pain they are in or the chaos they have created in their lives, mentally and physically, or in the lives of their loved ones.

For instance, we don't overeat unhealthy foods to attain poor health. And most who live unhealthy lifestyles do not think of themselves as being unwell. On the other hand, some of the least healthy people I've ever met were on restricted or fad diets. Of course, consuming too much food, overspending, or binge shopping creates physical issues, internal problems, diseases, or a predisposition for specific ailments. But that behavior does not define us. It is not a label we wear. It isn't who we are.

It's about that void we are trying to fill somewhere in our lives so deep we fill it with food, alcohol, or material goods to push down the pain. Life is often complicated, and it can be hard to be human. It's much easier to zone out and use whatever distraction we can to make ourselves feel better, even if it's unhealthy and temporary. Unfortunately, while it mostly numbs our pain, it also numbs our joy.

Part III

TRANSFORM

At this moment, you reflect on what you've accomplished.

Chapter Twenty-One

Why We Keep Holding On

That's all your house is—it's a place to keep your stuff while you go out and get more stuff. Now sometimes—sometimes, you gotta move. You gotta get a bigger house. Why? Too much stuff. You've gotta move all your stuff and maybe put some of your stuff in storage. Imagine that: There's a whole industry based on keeping an eye on your stuff.
—George Carlin, comedian

There are many reasons we hold on to things—material, emotional, and psychological. However, I've found that one of the most helpful practices for letting go of anything is to become more intentional with my goals when I want some transformation in my life. And this method applies whether I'm looking to donating items I haven't used in a while or letting go of people, old hurts and resentments, and other emotional baggage.

It's A Family Affair

There can be a lot of love, regret, and resentment around family, so I want to remind you, hey, there are no perfect families. And what does perfect even mean? Even the TV shows I grew up watching in the '70s and '80s depicted false representations of family. Yet, despite the façades we wear and contrary to what we see on social media, with everything carefully curated to show only the finished product—smiling faces, crisp and clean homes—coming from a dysfunctional family is the norm. We don't need or want to show that side to everyone, and we don't have to; that is our sacred space.

One of the ways family dynamics can build hurt and resentment is from what we believe our parents and extended family forced on us. Perhaps it is their unfulfilled dreams, or their unreachable expectations (whether real or perceived) of us. And whether we agree with those expectations, those dreams or not, we may still regret we did not live up to their ideals or that if we did follow in their footsteps, we feel we are not good enough. So even when we break out and make our way, we may still hold onto rebellion or defiance to define our choices.

I work with many families that holding on to stuff is not the issue when they get together to divide assets after a death in the family. Instead, estrangement and disconnect takes over as everyone fights over stuff even though they don't want it, just to make the others miserable. Either they want everything in the house and fight over certain items, or they don't want anything and then they call me to "just make it all go away." Sometimes when I'm in the house, I can feel how the painful memories linger.

However, a large majority of my clients grew up in cluttered homes, which is a key factor in why their own homes are also cluttered. And the piles and stacks only increased as family members grew up—more stress, more stuff, more need to fill that unfulfillable void. And then, when their parents pass away, the adult kids have even more stuff to deal with, and there it sits, and they sit with it, along with the guilt and responsibility.

For example, how can they throw away family photos or old marriage certificates? The decision to keep or donate or discard every piece of grandmother's wedding china, or the solid cherry dining room furniture that was a 25th wedding anniversary gift from their father to their mother, can be an agonizing one—whether their childhood was rocky or not.

After our parents passed away, my brothers and I had to look through stacks of photo albums. We only kept pictures of people we knew or recognized; otherwise, we threw them out. It broke my heart to throw away some of my parents' pictures and I hate filling up landfills.

I tell my clients we hardly look at family mementos we keep, and most of my clients never open the boxes of items from their parents' early years. It's fun to look at your own albums and books, but with no story behind the pictures in your parents' albums, why save them when you don't recognize anyone except them? If the picture has a changing landscape or is vintage, you can donate it to a local library or historical society. It may feel like we're disrespecting our parents, ancestry, or family, but unless you plan to write a book about your family history or have relatives who have indicated that they're interested in it, what other choice do we have?

If it helps, I am giving you permission to throw them away or donate them to a resale shop without feeling guilty.

Status, Insecurity, and Belonging

Status is another reason why we hold on to things. People keep buying and buying items they don't need because it makes them feel important and rich. Of course, it doesn't help that every day those images of perfection on social media inundate us in addition to the pressure to purchase the latest smartphone, fashion trend, appliance, and car. How much do we really need and how much money do we spend just to keep up a so-called perfect image?

The central theme is insecurity. Despite millions of years of evolution, we still desire and need to fit in and belong. There is subconscious fear, rooted in our primal brain, that if the tribe throws us out, we will die. But, unfortunately, this often-subconscious need to fit in, coupled with our fears around lack, scarcity, and belonging to groups drives many of us to want what "they" have. So, we shop to try to attain that status and seeming perfection. We shop to calm ourselves and soothe our insecurities. Continuing to live in denial, we are trapped in a loop of comparison and the proverbial "keeping up with the Joneses."

Many of my clients have storage units full of items they think they need and spend thousands of dollars a year to keep those things that they do not need or may never use. Somehow, it comforts them that "I have all this stuff that I don't need, and I have the money to keep it! That must mean I'm successful. I am successful. I can keep spending and spending and spending."

On a cellular level, this compulsion makes sense because acting this way does make us feel good—for that brief moment. All those yummy endorphins and feelings of satisfaction, completeness, and "richness" comfort us and make us feel safe and, more importantly, secure. Many of my clients feel lost inside. They assume that those who have stuff must be happy. How could they not be? They must be worthy, popular, fun, and smart because "they have everything," which translates to "the more stuff I have, the happier I will be, too."

But it's a lie. Isn't it?

When we feel inadequate just as we are, we fill our surroundings instead. And these insatiable feelings of need and fear also appear in other behaviors—too much food, too much alcohol, and being stuck in negative thoughts and toxic relationships. When all of the "space" gets cluttered—mentally and physically—life becomes overwhelming, smaller, and lonelier. The exact opposite of what we think people who "have it all" should feel.

This brutal cycle of buying too much, showing it off, feeling good for a moment, then feeling ashamed, and then buying more affects all types of people—status seekers, the insecure, or anyone just trying to fit in. It will continue until we decide (or life decides for us) to take an honest look at ourselves, reclaim our power, and do the work necessary to realize our worthiness, lovableness, and happiness dwell within us. Where we always belong.

Safety and comfort

In meeting people and helping them organize their homes, the most heartbreaking for me are clients who insulated themselves from the harsh and unforgiving outside world. For them, the more stuff they have, the safer they feel. No matter the size of their house, they fill it up, so there is less open—unprotected—space. Isolating themselves in a secluded cocoon reassures them that the world isn't that big. In their little world of comfort surrounded by things, they don't have to deal with anything on the outside. While they feel comfortable with everything they need right inside their little bubble, others would be claustrophobic and feel unhealthy.

It's similar to holding onto extra weight, something I discovered in my years as a personal trainer. Those extra pounds insulate us, protect us, and make us feel like no one will ever hurt us again. Physical weight and the "weight" of more stuff than we need can also give us a sense of security and a way to hide from the world. As a scheme to "guarantee" that no one will bother us or look at us, we also do not have to look at ourselves so closely.

However, using piles and piles of anything to find safety is another lie.

And while it may be true that no one will come looking for us in our tiny cocoon, we unconsciously lose our essential selves among our collections, hobbies, weight, and visual distractions. Surrounded by towers of boxes and papers, away from the shining sun and the sun of friendship and community, our hearts wither a little each day. Worse, the fear—that led us to build this fortress of extra—often buries us.

When I am lucky enough to work with someone in these cloistered situations, I show them they are loved, needed, and wanted and that there is purpose for their life. Regardless of what drives them to hold onto things, I meet every client with love, kindness, and respect, assuring them that they can move forward if they desire to make a change. I have such confidence in them because since they reached out for help, they will eventually trust and have more confidence in themselves. The ones who persevered in continuing with the complex work of inner healing while I worked shoulder to shoulder with them grew more comfortable with who they are—but there is a fine line. Yes, I am rooting for them and have confidence in their success; however, I know I cannot push them. They have to find that inner peace for themselves.

Remember that we will never be truly free until we commit to the inner work and ask ourselves why we hold onto material things, weight, past hurts, and family drama. Otherwise, the clutter will most likely return, and we will stay lost in our pain, not knowing why.

17
Spatulas

Chapter Twenty-Two

Making Room for a New Life

The more you love your decisions, the less you need others to love them.
—The Modern Savvy, "The More You Love Your Decisions"

I enjoy follow-up calls with clients when we have created a tight bond. For example, Peggy had been sick on and off. She was in her mid-70s and complained about pain in her side for a few months. When they found out what it was, she wasn't allowed to go up and down stairs until she recovered. So, as is typical for many of our clients who can't make stairs anymore, the family created a bedroom for her in the living room on the first floor. Since her disability had delayed us from starting her project, she was eager to start because, in a few months, her daughter would have the first grandchild in the family.

When Peggy scheduled the first consultation, she told me, "We have to get all of this sorting-out done because my daughter has warned me that otherwise, there might not be as many times of 'bringing baby over for a visit' as I am hoping." Her sister, Amy, was in town to help, so she was there when we arrived. And she proved invaluable, since Peggy could not be in the room with us to make decisions. Amy helped us declutter, acted as Peggy's eyes and ears, and aided as her emotional support. Sometimes the projects are very overwhelming, and this was one of them.

On the second floor, we focused on Peggy's bedroom and the attached room connected by French doors, which would be the baby's room. That first day, we could not even access the additional space. The bedroom had a path to the bed and one to the closet. In our first session, we threw out food containers, packages, leftovers, old papers, and tons of magazines and cleaned a lot.

In Peggy's nightstand drawers, we found jewelry, money, and receipts all mixed in with ketchup packets, change, cough drops, and old chicken bones. It looked like the drawer was opened, and someone had swept everything on top into the drawer. There were few emotional or big decisions to be made on what to keep and what to discard. We must have taken out sixteen trash bags before seeing what was underneath. That thick layer had been there for a very long time. With help from Peggy's sister, the Team Mentors worked hard and finished the project in plenty of time for the baby girl's arrival.

When I followed up with Peggy about three weeks after we finished, I asked her how she was doing health-wise and how she felt about the rooms we decluttered and organized.

Peggy said, "Oh my goodness! I'm so pleased with how your team and my sister cleaned everything up. It all looks amazing. I made it up there once to look but haven't slept there yet. I have to tell you, though, Lisa, when I went into the room, my first thought was, 'all my friends are gone?'"

I tilted my head, "What do you mean, Peggy?"

"It had all been with me for so long. I knew where everything came from, where I bought it, and who gave it to me. When I got sick the first time, this bedroom became all I had—life went on around me, and I just sat, ordered from online stores, watched TV, and ate. People brought me food, papers, and games. Lots of fast-food take-out, which I started craving. My family sat with me for meals, and the room became my solace."

It was heartbreaking to hear.

But Peggy felt a connection and had a relationship with what many people would label as "garbage" or "trash." In many ways, those things were her comfort and security. She said it took her a few days to get through the feeling of loss and abandonment. Remembering her goal helped her tremendously.

Then she said something I had never heard a client admit. It was almost like she was admitting it to herself rather than me. She said, "Lisa,

I am a hoarder. I know that now. This process was very challenging, especially since I could not be in the room with you. I know they all had to go, all my friends. I also know what is in store for me. My grandbaby can come here, and I'm very excited about that!"

It is normal for a client to begin a project like this one and get to a point where they question why they're even doing it. The payoff in not doing anything about clearing up a space is to stay in their comfort zone. So, what is the payoff for committing to organizing and clearing out? A better question is, "What am I making room for?" In Peggy's case, her commitment to making room for her grandchild helped her transcend the unhealthy connection to her things.

My job with Peggy was extraordinary because I felt so trusted and honored to be able to work for her benefit and well-being without her even being in the room with us. Also, it was the first time I realized the deep, emotional connection clients could have to their things—even if it just looks like trash to the outside world.

By decluttering, Peggy made room for a literal new life. Her vision for that new life motivated her to step out of the comfort she had felt in her bedroom—and began a new phase in her life.

17
Spatulas

Chapter Twenty-Three

Identity and Possible Selves

Your space is a reflection of your mental health. The more disorganized and cluttered, the more internal anxiety, depression, and fear we have.
—Cyndi Turner

I've created the term "lifers"—people who have lived in their homes a long time and haven't thrown out much of anything for years. They have a method we recognize when we go into their homes to help manage their space. All the trash bags go there. They stack all the newspapers over here, all the empty plastic containers are in this place, and the canned foods are in another. They have certain rooms they stack their unopened clothes, and they know where everything is. That is their idea of organizing—while it's not healthy or functional, sometimes there truly is a method to the madness.

I've also worked with clients who say they have been organized in the past and are trying to organize again. When I arrive for a consultation, they say, "I used to have such a clean home. You can't tell now, but I was so organized. I like how I feel when I am organized. It calms me, and I feel prepared for anything."

I respond confidently. "Well, that tells me you can be organized again. We will find what works for you now in your life and space. Lives change. You're not the same person you were when you were that uber-organized person."

People who are adamant in their decision to get organized have a firm conviction and intention. They buy organizing tools, books, and containers, which are all good intentions—just like New Year's resolutions. How about getting fit as a New Year's resolution? You purchase a gym membership and plan to start on Monday. The idea sounds great because it lets you be someone you have always wanted to be. You want to be that healthy, physically active person. The membership gets you the first step; the rest you need to do—actually go to the gym. Many say, "I need to take this step to achieve this goal to become this person. Now what? I have the right tools, so why isn't anything changing for the better?"

One particular client owned fourteen vacuums intending to keep her house clean. She identified herself as a person who kept a pristine home. "This is who I want to be: I am a clean and tidy person. See, I have vacuums and cleaning products and all the paraphernalia." It symbolizes for them someone they want to be and could be. "I am taking control of my space and life by cleaning."

Definition and Characterization of Possible Selves

Possible selves, coined by Hazel Markus and Paula Nurius, are described as how individuals think about their potential and future. They think of an individual's possible self as the cognitive link between past experiences and future hopes, desires, fears, and fantasies.

Alleydog.com defines the term, Possible Selves as referring to various components of the cognitive sense of self; the ideal self (who a person would like to be), who they can become, and even perhaps who they might be afraid of becoming.

My client with 14 vacuums is afraid of becoming someone who lives in an unclean and disorganized space. Her decision to buy these vacuums was emotional, not logical, because logically, why would you buy more stuff if you're trying to be more organized and become that "clean" person? So first, you need to get rid of the things you don't want. Then figure out what you need, if anything, to stay organized and clean.

However, we are not logical when we're stuck and coming from an emotional state. When we feel this way, we don't feel worthy or successful. We don't feel loved or supported and need to prove something.

To hijack this way of thinking, we must accept why these feelings and emotions are coming up. What is the emotion driving the behavior? When you're happy, you sit in it and enjoy it. When you're sad, you sit in it and cry. Choose to do the same thing with all your emotions.

My friend, Craig James, said it best: "If you had a broken foot and went to step on it, you would feel pain. It would probably be excruciatingly painful, yes? Do you ignore it? Can you dismiss it? How could you? No, you honor it; you treat it and get help. You listen to it to figure out how to take care of it and heal it. You treat the 'why.' Why am I doing what I'm doing? Why am I feeling what I'm feeling? Sit with it and find healing. That's the only way to make the changes you need and want in your life."

So, sit with your feelings—don't run from them. Because once you can accept and acknowledge the emotion and where you're at, you can do something about it. But if you keep pushing it down with stuff, feeling like something is wrong with you, or completely dismissing the feelings, your chances of healing and changing decrease.

An Outward Representation of Inner Pain

My therapist friend, Dianne, shared the heartbreaking story of a woman she worked with when she was still an intern with an agency that made house calls. Dianne believes, and I do as well, the amount of visual clutter is equal to the degree of someone's pain. She walked into her client's house and almost immediately wanted to turn around to leave. "I have never seen visually the extent of how much pain someone could be inside. She looked so tiny among all the clutter. There wasn't an inch of space—I had to turn and scoot around. The toilet barely worked, and she hadn't showered in quite a long time."

An intense and extreme degree of desperation oozed from her client. She could not bring one more thing into her home or her mind—stuff filled every crevice. In addition, the woman was Agoraphobic (an anxiety disorder characterized by a fear of particular places and situations that the person believes are difficult to escape, such as open spaces and public transport). She was a hermit, had numerous health concerns, and could hardly walk.

Dianne admitted, "Lisa, it was so overwhelming to sit with her and be with her. I struggled to stay focused enough to figure out how best to help her. It was so clear the tremendous pain this woman was in because of the amount of stuff. I don't know how you do it." Her client used to work in a high-end shoe store, and she would buy shoes with every paycheck. Dianne recalled at least 900 pairs of new, unused shoes in boxes around the home. They were encrusted with a thick layer of dust and rodent droppings.

"I could see dead mice and rats under and around the boxes." She paused. "It struck me while we were talking how much she desperately wanted to be that person wearing these fabulous shoes. How will I look when I wear these shoes? Where would I go? What would people think when they saw me? What does that say about me to own and wear these fancy shoes? It was the dream of who she could be while in those shoes."

She was stockpiling missed opportunities of dreams with misguided attempts to self-soothe—it would never be enough. More shoes soothe the pain for a while, but after a short time, it wears off, and she needs another fix.

You should dress for the success you want (within your budget, of course). I know that when I'm walking around in sweatpants or workout clothing, I don't feel like I would be ready to go in front of a group of people and teach or conduct a presentation. It just doesn't feel appropriate to be in comfy clothing instead of more professional attire. I feel different when I wear a gown and high heels and put on makeup—very powerful. But changing your clothing, driving an expensive car, or living in a big house does not change who you are or how you feel about yourself, especially deep inside. People do look at you differently and may treat you differently because of the car you drive and your neighborhood. I guess that is the goal for some people. But when it comes down to it, you have to know who you are and why you do what you do—because you are not your stuff.

I worked with a very insightful and intelligent gentleman one day.

As Anthony looked at ALL his stuff, he started saying, "I am *not* my stuff, *I* am not my stuff! I am not my *stuff!*"

At first, I giggled a bit because I thought he was being silly. But then we started talking about it, and I thought about the comment. "Maybe this is it. Do people have so much stuff to make themselves feel good? Feel vital? Feel powerful? Feel successful? Worthy, even?"

Why does the need for and acquiring "stuff" help us believe those things? Can we be as impressive to our neighbors by having less stuff? And why do we have to impress our neighbors? Living with less stuff gives us more time, space, and freedom.

I say impress yourself from within. After all, you are not your stuff.

17 "
Spatulas

Chapter Twenty-Four

Reaching a Plateau

About five months into his decluttering project, Vince greeted me with a big smile and a fresh cup of coffee in his hand. "Well, hello, Lisa! Would you like a cup before we start?"

We both knew it was time to tackle the upstairs—procrastination was over. Doing all of his homework, Vince felt inspired and excited about the potential for himself and his home—his energy had shifted. The time had arrived. He rubbed his hands eagerly. "Okay, let's do this. Coffee's made, and I have fruit, snacks, and tissues, just in case. Don't stop until we get to the landing."

He was ready. The day before, we had an extra group call with his therapist to help him prepare, which did the trick.

"I'll grab the garbage bags and empty boxes, and we'll get moving," I said as I placed a recently resurrected dining chair at the bottom of the stairs for Vince to sit on.

From the items I brought down off the steps leading to the third floor, he sorted into boxes for papers to keep, donations, recycling, or just plain garbage. Three hours went by quickly, with few challenging decisions for him to make. Finally, wrinkling his nose at a pile of old papers and mail, he said, "It's all so old and icky, no need to even look at it." While this stuff was easy, it was the warm-up—the more complex work was to come.

When I finally got up the stairs to the landing, I cheered from the top, and he cheered from the bottom. "Wow, we did it!"

"You made it happen, Lisa!"

I joined him on the main floor, and after a short break, Vince said, "I could do more. How about you?"

Even though I was exhausted from many trips up the steps and bringing loads of stuff down, his enthusiasm helped me catch my second wind. "Let's do it!" Then, I grabbed the vacuum, working it up the stairs and across the landing. However, I was blocked again, so I cleared a pathway in the short hallway leading to three bedrooms and a bathroom.

Vince made his way up the cleared stairs, and I could hear him remarking in a soft voice what a difference it made.

I watched Vince timidly walk toward me through the piles of stuff to sit. To keep our momentum going, I started with the bathroom as the least emotional and most straightforward for him to go through, considering he had not ventured onto this floor of his home for years.

He took command. "Keep the organizing bins, donate the lamp, recycle the huge box of old office phones. Oh, these empty file boxes, we can use them and keep two of the twenty new packages of printer paper."

When we finished the bathroom, Vince was ready to continue. He peeked into the second bedroom that he once used for his office. The desk was piled high with papers, boxes, and extras of this and that. Shelves lined the room, all filled and jammed with books, documents, and files. Awards, medals, and pictures hung on the walls from his military career. Vince had also saved trophies and memories from his successful career as an entrepreneur and business owner. He needed to see, remember, and keep some prominent items that symbolized all he had accomplished. These positive memories reinforced his feelings of having a good life. He and I were so proud of the seventy percent he donated or recycled and had shredded out of that room.

This process of sorting, making decisions, and clearing out is mentally and physically exhausting for all involved. It's emotionally draining to make decisions about thousands and thousands of belongings, even for everyday items. For deciding on personally meaningful objects, it's best to have shorter sessions with more breaks, with easier decisions mixed in.

Understandably, most people don't want to tackle the sorting out process alone in their homes. It's one of the reasons why I have a business. I take time and have the patience to help people find their determination to make it through to the other side, where they will feel lighter physically, mentally, and emotionally.

17
Spatulas

Part IV

LOVE IT & LIVE IT!

You've identified those items you love and choose
to keep in your world, which is now focused
and less cluttered physically and mentally.

Chapter Twenty-Five

Toasting to a New Life

One of the greatest regrets in life is being what others
would want you to be rather than being yourself.
—Shannon L. Alder

The phone rang, and with a strong southern accent, a woman's fierce voice asked, "How do you deal with an a-hole husband's stuff who just leaves it, his wife and family, for another woman?"

Stunned, shocked, and intrigued, I said, "Well if it's worth anything, let's sell it and make you some money."

I heard her take a deep breath. "Great! What's the earliest you can start?"

I arranged to meet her at her house the following morning.

As I drove my minivan up the meandering driveway, eventually presenting a stately colonial that was easily 6,000 square feet, a stunningly beautiful, tall blonde opened the garage door and approached my car, exactly as I imagined her from her voice. She was clutching what I assumed was a cup of coffee.

I hopped out, gave her my card, and held out a hand. "Arlene? I'm Lisa. We spoke yesterday."

She took my hand in a soft grip at odds with her strident voice and nodded. "Mornin', Lisa, nice to meet y'all. Ready to get this party started?"

I laughed, thrilled to have a client full of energy and ready to go. But I felt her sadness and hesitancy as well.

We walked through the three-car garage that had one spot open. Two wave runners filled the second space, and occupying the third was a mix of bikes, snow and water skies, and various sports equipment.

She turned to me as we entered the large and sunny kitchen. "Can I get you a cup of coffee, hon?"

I hadn't had time to grab my morning latte, so I accepted with a smile. "So, Arlene, tell me what's going on."

She didn't need any further prompting. "Sorry, I was a little off my rocker yesterday because the damn divorce papers came. I guess I've been holding a little hope these last three years that he'd come back. But that right there broke my heart and pissed me right off all over again. Walter, my ex, was my high school sweetheart. Grew up together." She smiled sadly. "Sounds like a movie, right? Then, three summers ago, before the twins went to college, I took them to Savannah to visit our families. Walter had to stay and work, or so he said. When we returned a week later, he and most of his clothes were gone. He left all of his other crap behind—he was so eager to move in with his new piece, my former best friend. Can you believe it? His family had no idea either, so they say."

"Holy cats," I said, my eyes wide as saucers. "Can't make that up!"

"I asked everyone I knew and finally located him at my girlfriend's house. Only now, she was his girlfriend. He had moved in with her. Into the condo that I helped her buy. Wasn't that convenient?" Her voice was harsh and stern, but the pain was still raw and saturated every ounce of her being.

"So, why are you ready now?" I asked.

"The kids aren't coming back to this house, and it's way too big for me. I've just been too busy, but now I'm finally ready to move, and I've been sitting with all his stuff for too long." Shaking her head, she added, "As I said, I have been holding out hope he would come back. He didn't last more than a year with Suzanne, my ex-friend. And then he shacked up with someone else." She spoke with a twinge of sadness.

———————

Arlene and I worked once a week for two months, focusing on her physical stuff. She was also in therapy, which I recommend to anyone, especially when dealing with trauma. So much anger and grief came up for her that the extra support was the best mixture.

Her therapist told her that forgiveness is significant when it comes to letting go. The first step is to forgive yourself. For "procrastinating," for "now needing help," for "not knowing where to start," for "not being perfect." Holding on to regrets, resentments, and past mistakes keeps us stuck in a loop of our own making. When we practice compassion toward ourselves, it makes it a little easier to practice it toward others.

Forgiveness of those who have hurt us or left their stuff for us to deal with is also essential if we are to transform our lives. Forgiving them does not absolve any wrongdoing on their part. Instead, it is for our peace and health. Chances are the person or persons who hurt you won't even remember the story or the situation.

After those two months, Arlene was finally ready to deal with her ex-husband's stuff and understood enough was enough. We brought all his belongings to the garage and added them to the bigger items. She arranged a time window for him to come when she would be away for a few hours. He was to come and get everything out; otherwise, she would sell it, donate it or throw it out. When she returned, it was all gone—everything.

The next day when I arrived, I asked gently, "How do you feel?"

"The young, hopeful me is absolutely devastated, and all the old feelings came up when I opened the garage and saw it was empty. All the pain, hurt, and sorrow came flooding through me again. It took me a while to be ready to create this change. And it took me some time to process. I think I'm still a little numb today. But last night, that crazy expensive bottle of wine we found helped a lot."

We teased and giggled through the pain and truth of her comments. That time in her life was over; he had been physically gone from her and her children's lives for years. Now, she knew he didn't rule her anymore. She was ready to move on with her life.

"I finally feel free and relieved with a sense of calm I have never felt before. I've made peace with all my worries and regrets about even marrying him in the first place. There was no mistake. I have two beautiful, healthy children from that marriage. And you know what? I can buy that bright pink couch he always made fun of that I've always wanted. And no more holidays at my ex-mother-in-law's who can't cook for love or money!"

I laughed, adding, "Your kids needed you, and you fulfilled your promise. You are the mom they needed and wanted, and you played both roles. I trust your kids came out ahead and are stronger because of you. It's better to have one solid, wonderful single parent than two married people who are dysfunctional and make life extremely difficult for themselves and everyone around them."

"I'll toast to that." She laughed, and we raised imaginary glasses to her new future.

17
Spatulas

Chapter Twenty-Six

The Significance of an Object

It's okay to be scared. Being scared means you're about to do something really, really brave.
—Mandy Hale, *The Single Woman:*
Life, Love, and a Dash of Sass

When I was seven, my dad gave me a special birthday present. What made it so special was that I knew Dad had picked it out this time—whereas Mom usually had that role. And secondly, Dad made a big deal out of it by making sure his gift was my last one to receive. He looked so proud and took loving care as he gently handed me a colored box. My mom didn't know what it was, so I knew that my dad had seen this item himself and bought it for me.

Inside the gift box was a small wooden shelf with miniature copper kitchen pots and pans made to hang on the little hooks and sit on the shelf. I was thrilled. At that time, I remember loving anything small I could play with in my imaginary world. Immediately we found a place on a wall in my bedroom that was perfect for my special little gift. I rearranged the pots and pans and played with them daily for a very long time. It sits on my shelf in my office today. And with my dad's passing in 2009, it is even more precious to me.

We keep things that hold special memories for us and tell a story. Truly honor these special memories—don't allow them to sit forgotten in some drawer or box, gathering dust. The work of sorting and purging is more than simply making room for more stuff or throwing things out. It's learning to love the things we own and live with them in a way that makes our space—mentally and physically—feel comfortable and calm.

Knowing Your Why

I met a young woman named Andrea at an event, and when we started a conversation about organizing, she told me how she loved it but still needed some help. "I'm fairly organized," she began, "however, I have a stack of *Sports Illustrated* magazines in one corner of my living room that I can't get rid of, and I don't know why."

She went on to explain that it was her younger brother's subscription. They had lived together, and it was his favorite magazine; he was really into all sports and always had their TV turned to some sports event. On the other hand, Andrea didn't like sports, never played, and never enjoyed them, being more into the theater and the arts.

"I've kept up my brother's subscription to the magazine after he passed away in a car accident at 26. It was so devastating. It's only been three years, seems like more, and I just haven't gotten around to canceling it."

When I came over to her brick townhouse in Old Towne Alexandria the following week, she described how things had changed. "I would come home after a long day of work, and his big TV was always on and loud, of course, tuned to some violent boxing or hockey tournament. I just wanted to come home and relax, so when I came home to all that noise after a long day—" She paused, her breath hitching. "—I wished I lived alone." She paused again, took a deep breath, and let it out. "Now, it's so silent when I come home—what I always wanted. But, sometimes, I turn on the sports channel to fill the emptiness."

Andrea told me that she and her brother had always been close and became even more so after moving away from a small town in Iowa for college and work. She laughed as she told me, "It's funny, he absolutely loved sports, but he could never play any very well because he just wasn't very coordinated." She shook her head and laughed some more.

As we sat in front of the stack of magazines, I suggested she try one of the techniques I use for my clients when they have piles of papers, newspapers, or clothing.

"Turn the pile over so what was on the bottom is now on top. That way, you start looking at things that are the oldest, easiest to assess, and potentially to let go. That method also gives us answers and insights into how long the stack has been sitting there, taking up precious space mentally and physically."

When Andrea turned the stack over, tears filled her eyes as she realized the first issue was the month and year of her brother's passing. We both got goosebumps and just stared at each other and then at the pile and back at each other again.

I was speechless and knew that, in this moment, there was so much power and healing for her.

"That explains so much," she said through her tears.

We just sat there looking at it, eventually smiling.

Then, Andrea started sharing different, funny memories of her brother, which generated more tears and laughter—healing and cathartic.

I proposed that she keep the first issue and recycle or donate the rest of the collection. She agreed that she could do that and said this realization and decision made a vast and powerful impact on how she felt. It brought her brother back to her differently, and she could remember even more of the good stuff. That pile of magazines had been a visual reminder that her brother had passed, eating her up inside, and she didn't even know it. Andrea will always miss him. However, keeping the magazines would never bring her brother back. It was the right time for her to let them go and move on.

Respect the Value of "LITL" Things

When I work with a client, I love hearing stories about their lives and stuff. I learn so much about their past, how much they have overcome and grown, and how they have enjoyed their lives. As I keep saying, it's important to keep the things that mean something to you. The positive things remind you of the past and will keep you feeling good in the future. We all have objects of significance that we become attached to, so the challenge becomes knowing what to keep to move you on positively and what to let go of—what's holding you back negatively from the past.

I was at a friend's birthday party and started talking to Ray, sitting alone at a table. When he discovered I was a professional organizer, he told me he had worked with an organizer to help him move after his wife passed about ten years earlier. He and his wife had traveled the world and collected little treasures along the way. They had boxed up many of the items in different closets and places around the house, and he hadn't seen them for a very long time.

Most of my clients admit that some items are easy to sort through and decide whether to keep or discard. Then there are those more challenging items, mementos, pictures, and small items of impact, playing a significant part in their history. For example, he told me the story about this little statue of the Eiffel Tower they bought on their trip to Paris.

He laughed. "To look at it, it wasn't anything too special—we bought it from one of those touristy vendors on the Avenue des Champs-Elysees. Debbie just fell in love with the statue, so I bought it for her. She had it up on a shelf in our bedroom for years but boxed it up when we had the room repainted, and the shelf didn't go up again. I don't think I'd seen it since then until the organizer opened the box when we worked together. When she saw it, she immediately put it in the donation pile. Luckily, I saw her do it, so I reached for it and said, 'I would like to keep that if it's okay. Can I have it back?' Her response to me was, 'Why would you keep it? It looks kind of cheap.' And she put it back in the donation pile."

I stared at him; my mouth open. As an organizer, I see my client's trust in me as an honor and a sacred responsibility. Just because I'm an expert in organizing has nothing to do with what's important to you. I cannot reiterate the purpose of this role enough—an organizer is there as a guide, someone to brainstorm and discuss the items you have and why they're meaningful to you. Some clients ask me outright, "What should I do?" And when that happens, we discuss it further.

Sadly, I've heard this type of story more than once. All I can say is, give yourself permission to disagree with your organizer. They will not take it personally if they're honestly there to help you. They must treat your space and your items with respect and discuss any donations or trash with you before you make a decision. I emphasize the need for my clients to take these steps themselves—while I serve as an objective guide.

Ray had tears in his eyes as he said, "That was, gosh, it has to be ten years ago now, and I still remember it, and it still breaks my heart. I feel like I let my wife down somehow because I didn't speak up."

I put my hand on his hand to ease some of his pain.

We can only hope another couple found the Eiffel Tower at a second-hand store, fell in love with it, and now have it on a shelf in their home, still spreading joy.

Acknowledge Your Feelings and Trust Your Decision

Miriam had lived in her house for over thirty years, when I met her, her kids had moved out, and her husband had passed away a few years before. She still missed him terribly, and when she realized she wanted to move closer to her grandchildren, she needed help downsizing and preparing to move to a warmer climate. As we walked through her house, Miriam told me which child slept in which room and how she had made all their drapes, comforters, and pillows to each child's liking. She shared the many memories they made in those rooms and many significant events that had taken place.

"Garry and Anna are taking certain pieces of furniture and various artwork, but I don't want to take much to the new apartment." When we entered the main bedroom, she stopped and gazed at the queen-size bed set, a sad smile on her smooth brown face. "It took us almost sixteen months to save up for this bed set. We made a lot of memories here. The kids loved being read to in here on stormy nights."

"Do you think you will keep it?" I asked.

"I can't decide what to do," she said. "My kids want me to keep it. It reminds them of the nights we and our Doberman, Stash, would pile on it after watching scary movies. But they don't want it because there's no room in their smaller homes or it doesn't match their decor."

I nodded. "It is comforting to see familiarity after a loss. How do you feel looking at it?"

Miriam tilted her head. "While I know it's beautiful, and I think it would be okay to bring it, I feel sad and lonely when I look at it. I feel horrible that I will let down my kids because they want me to keep it, and I feel guilty that I don't want it. I don't want to betray the memory of my husband. And I don't want them to think I'm bad because I don't want to take it with me. But if I don't, my children might forget all the good memories associated with that set."

I looked at her and touched her on the arm. "Miriam, it sounds like your kids had an amazing relationship with their dad—I don't think they'll ever forget him, even if you sell or donate the set. What truly matters is how you feel about it and whether you think it belongs in this next phase of your life."

That day, Miriam decided not to take a bedroom set with her to her new home. For the new chapter in her life, she realized she needed to let go of a cherished possession that was just too painful for her. This decision enabled her to move forward without regrets and know and trust that her husband was proud of her decision because all he wanted was for her to be happy.

Sometimes, the significance of an item is so great that we want to save it to pass on to the next generation or two. If you decide to do this, take some time to pick out a few special things that you would like to give to your children and grandchildren. Write a little note about how you came to have the item, a little story behind it, and why you want that person to have it. If you can be with that person, ask them first, tell them why you want them to have it, and give it to them now—the connection will be even stronger. Don't wait.

Make Your Own Rules

Here in Northern Virginia, we have had mild winters. Therefore, if we take the rule "if you haven't worn it in a year, get rid of it," seriously, everyone would have to buy new winter apparel. It's been over a year since many of us have worn our heavy boots and outerwear! That's one of the reasons I don't have that rule or any "organizing rules."

Growing up in the suburbs of Chicago and then living downtown for almost two decades, I know about the loss of feeling in my face and extremities. While owning my fitness company, I would fight the elements trying hard not to slip on ice to get from client to client and crossing the Chicago River on Lake Shore Drive, just getting to my car from the gym. Finally, one year I broke down and bought a shearling coat a size too big because I would have on my silks layer, sweatpants, sweatshirt, a warmer sweater or jacket, and then the shearling. With thick socks and heavy boots, double gloves, double scarves—one around my neck to cover my face—and a shearling hat, two eyeballs were all the evidence that a human being was way back behind all that.

I have clients, friends, and myself included, who don't necessarily wear every piece of clothing each season, so does that mean I need to buy a new wardrobe each year? How about our formalwear, books on our shelves, china, glassware, silver, and the "special occasion" stuff? Or the knickknacks, mementos, pictures, and the history that goes along with them?

When we work with our clients, we never talk them into getting rid of something (unless they insist that we do, in which case they probably didn't want it anyway). We have no idea of the significance something has had on their life. We ask questions, listen to the stories, and will be content with whatever the outcome. If they want to keep it, they keep it. Our clients have come to a place where they need additional help to clear the clutter, make room for the next phase of their lives, or sort through things they don't want to pay to move again—it is not our place to judge.

17
Spatulas

Chapter Twenty-Seven

Facing His Worst Fear

"Good morning, Lisa." Vince greeted me for our next session. He wanted to start in the bedroom office with his awards on the walls. With full bookshelves piled high lining one wall, this room served more like a closet and storage room. There were boxes of books and papers throughout the room, and then on top of those were layers of brand-new clothing. The clothing was still in bags he had ordered years ago online or bought at one of the membership stores.

"I used to be organized. You'd never believe it now, but I was. Dad was very strict. Wanted everything to be in order." Vince always had a goal and a dream to organize his belongings. "I want to be that organized person living in a clean and happy home. I know it is a possibility for me."

"You're definitely on the right track Vince. And it's never too late," I said encouragingly. "Once we have out what you don't want, we will find a place for what you want to keep and create a plan to keep it organized." And then I opened the closet door, which had been closed, and my jaw dropped. Vince had super organized everything inside! I turned to look at him, smiling from ear to ear.

"Oh, I forgot how good I was." He snickered. He had labeled and categorized his old college memorabilia, family albums, and pictures in plastic bins. We had a good laugh at the sight of this collection, and he blushed for an hour!

Vince's homework for this room was sorting the clothing in the boxes to see if he wanted to keep any of it and if he could fit in the pants and shirts. Most of the clothes were still in pretty good shape. We set up numerous piles of Yes, No, and Maybe. He also had new clothes draped over the boxes to sort through. Finally, we sorted through the books and memorabilia he wanted to keep. Vince was on a roll.

———————

Two days later, I arrived to: "Happy Friday, Lisa." Again, Vince's enthusiasm was contagious.

"Top of the morning there, Vince." Walking into a bright and cheery living space was so glorious. I knew he felt the same. But this morning, his eyes were bloodshot from a night of tossing and turning. "Vince, what happened? Are you Okay?"

"Today is the day, isn't it?"

"Only if you want it to be. It is the last room."

He grinned sideways and went into the kitchen.

I made my way upstairs and placed his work chair outside the main bedroom he had once shared with his wife. Creedence Clearwater Revival's "Down on the Corner" started blasting from below, along with a louder voice over the music, "Just so you know, I'm procrastinating down here. Want some coffee? Making a fresh pot!"

Laughing at his reclaimed and lighter personality, I yelled, "Sure," and started singing along as I stood in the hall looking into the bedroom I could barely walk into, hands on hips. Then, I got to work, setting up the boxes for recycling and opening up the pack of garbage bags.

It's best to start at the edge of the abyss for a monumental task like this one. Work your way in, one piece at a time. With another look over the stacks and stacks of books, papers, and magazines blocking the entrance, I took a deep breath and began. I knew it would take over an hour before I could take even a few steps into the room. The sheer volume of stuff in this room surprised me. It looked like someone turned a storage container upside down that exploded. I could see books, paper, and newspapers thrown all over, as well as magazines, clothing, kitchen items, and shoes, even brand-new tools that belonged in a garage or shed.

Music was still blaring, and no sign of Vince yet, so I worked quickly to make some progress before he came upstairs.

Soon I heard a light clearing of the throat. Vince appeared and stood outside the room, peering inside with dejection filling his bright eyes. He raised an eyebrow, looked down, and moved the chair further along the hallway, not ready to even sit outside the door. Before Vince entered the room, I knew I had to work alone, discarding old newspapers and magazines, recycling, and removing full garbage bags. He handed me a cup of coffee and disappeared back downstairs. I continued working.

Six garbage bags full, three boxes of recycling, and two hours later, I headed downstairs to the main floor, making a few trips to set everything outside by my vehicle to take away that day after our session. Then I stretched and took in full deep breaths of fresh air before I walked back into the house to find Vince in the kitchen where the CCR concert was still playing. "Have You Ever Seen the Rain?" I wanted to see that Vince was okay because I hadn't seen him for a while. Vince had a sandwich, salad, and drink set at a now-clear table where we could both sit and enjoy. Good timing!

"What's this about, Vince?"

"Well, to avoid going into that room, which I know is inevitable, I decided to treat you to lunch at Chez Vincenzo's. I've been working and working all morning for you. Just a small way to say how much I appreciate you and thank you for your commitment to me in this big mess I've created."

We sat down for a lovely lunch and a much-needed talk. "What's the scariest part, Vince?"

He hesitated, and then the floodgates opened. "I am not a weak man. My dad taught me to be strong. To be a man's man and to always take care of things. Never let anyone see you doubt yourself. If someone takes advantage of you, you strike back. You take care of it!" He was struggling with breath and words but continued fearlessly. "She did that to me. She made me weak. I gave her everything, and I lost myself in her. In my love for her and my devotion, and when she took advantage, stole, cheated, and lied, I let her for so long. I thought I had no choice. She gaslighted me so well and convinced me I wasn't man enough."

I pulled my chair next to him and wrapped my arms around him as he collapsed into me. He felt so tiny and, at the same time, as heavy as an anchor. What should I say? What could I do? Nothing. Absolutely nothing. I am not a licensed therapist. All I could do was be there and listen.

He finally sat up and said, "Damn, I had no idea that would come up from inside of me. I am so sorry if this emotion is too much for you. I had no idea it was even in my thoughts. That was really deep in there, huh? Wow, just wow. I need an extra session with my therapist this week. What do you think? Because I am a man and a damn good one." And with that, he stood up and made his way up the cleared-off stairs to the second floor. I followed diligently.

Together, we stood for a moment at the doorway of the bedroom he once shared with his wife. From what I had cleared out so far, I could see that Vince's side of the bed was still ruffled and unmade from the last night he had slept there. A pair of eyeglasses and a coffee mug with a science experiment in it sat atop a tower of books on his nightstand. The far side of a room is always the first to get stuffed with items thrown absentmindedly and mixed into the massive mess of whatever was there before. I could tell he tried to sleep on his side of the bed for a while after his wife left. Eventually, her side of the bed became another space to release his anger—piling it high with food containers, magazines, newspapers, and trash. However, trashing her side left him with even less space to sleep. Eventually, with so many piles, the walls closed in on him, and the entire room became suffocating and unbearable, especially in his misery.

"Okay, let's get to work," he finally said with determination.

I set up a new staging area with his work chair in the other bedroom, bringing items for him to go through. Easy things: more books, office supplies, clothing. He sorted, purged, and kept up with the pace until I checked in with him and noticed his eyes had glassed over.

"Okay, Vince, you've been at it two hours. Let's call it a day. I'll finish up in the other room and meet you downstairs."

He nodded and headed down.

17
Spatulas

Chapter Twenty-Eight

Choose Discomfort

One of the things I talk a lot about in my work that I try to practice—
which is really hard—is in those moments where we're being asked to do
things or asked to take over or asked to take care of something, we have to
have the courage to choose discomfort over resentment. And to me, a huge
part of my authenticity practice has been choosing discomfort and saying no.
—Brené Brown

We all desire to feel safe, secure, and comfortable where we live. However, when we live with someone who has a lot of stuff (or if we have a lot of stuff), it's easier to turn a blind eye and stay in a comfort zone of denial. There comes the point where you don't want to bring up the fact that there's too much stuff. But avoiding the issue means we end up with less and less room to move around, which isn't healthy and gets uncomfortable too. And ignoring the problem helps neither the person holding on to too much stuff nor the person living with them.

If the clutter in your home affects you first thing every morning and all day long, it's time to reconsider moving out of your comfort zone and addressing the situation. Hopefully, there is openness and trust within the relationship for you to feel comfortable suggesting improvements. It's not about calling somebody out on their clutter. Instead, it's about coming from love and how much you care about them and are willing to help them live in a healthier, simpler environment. Make sure they know you care deeply for their health, safety, and well-being.

When we don't acknowledge or mention that a loved one is living in an unhealthy environment, we enable them to continue putting themselves in harm's way. Help them look at the situation from a different view. Are there any hazards? Electric cords covered, high stacks that can fall, outlets and vents, or other slip hazards, like loose area rugs? People who surround themselves with too much stuff are putting themselves and anyone else in the home in a precarious situation. It's an accident waiting to happen. And if you don't reach out and help, and something does happen, the guilt will be enormous. So, take the risk, and speak up kindly and gently. Start with small steps.

The first step is to get out of your comfort zone and offer to help and support your friends and family.

Choosing Discomfort for Ourselves

When we have lived in a space for years and years, we stop seeing much of anything, let alone how cluttered it has become. But believe it or not, there is some comfort in a full nest. When I go into a relative's home or the home of one of my mom's neighbors, there's a familiarity there when everything is as it was before. People get comfortable in their space and don't want to change.

Having clutter may feel easy! Keeping the status quo is easy—not making changes feels safe. On the other hand, getting organized takes effort, determination, and time. It's much easier to avoid it and not deal with the stuff, let alone try to get and stay organized. "It's been disappointing in the past; I don't want to do that again. It hurts. And I don't like it." And then you buy a third or fourth shovel because you can never find the other two you already bought. Or you would like to invite friends over, but you have nowhere to put the stash of cases of extra-large boxes of macaroni and cheese, toilet cleaner, or economy pack of paper towels you just had to have because they were on sale. And now, choosing instead to cancel the invitation, you suddenly feel more isolated and alone—with your stuff.

Once you've reached the point where you're ready to unpack some of the "boxes" in your life—physical or mental—the best way to approach it is to set a small goal, keep going, and take regular breaks. Some "boxes" are more straightforward to go through than others because each "box" holds a different degree of challenge. It is not always pleasurable to go through the items we've held onto, or someone gave us. We often don't look forward to it, and it can get, hmm—complicated.

Think of the commercial tagline "just do it." Over the years, that expression has made me cringe because not everybody can "just do" something. So, when I would talk about The LITL System and say, "You just have to start," or "You just have to decide," I realized, hey, it's not always that easy. Not everyone can accomplish something by JUST doing it. You need help to go through your stuff; you need the courage to reach out for that help. And first, you need to want to make this change, create a plan to do it, and then make the time to start.

You can begin with one decision. "Justing" doesn't work for everyone.

What is the price you pay by not making that time to start? Not taking control? To continue to sit and wait? Do you not invite people over, sleep on the couch or the floor, or order take-out every night because you can't cook in your kitchen?

If there are lots of papers and magazines in your home, there will be an overabundance of dust, which creates a health hazard for everyone living there. Full basements and garages have mice and rats, which is detrimental to your health. There is always a price for holding on to stuff instead of moving on—sometimes, it is monetary. But more importantly, the price is your health, physical well-being, and peace of mind.

Look at The LITL System again. Let go of what you know you don't want, make some intentional decisions for the rest, and that's it. It is simple. That doesn't mean it's easy. If it were easy, I wouldn't have a career, and we wouldn't need to be there to help people make those decisions.

The Discomfort of Changing Habits

Here are a few questions: Which foot do you put your sock on first each day? Which pant leg do you start with, left or right? And how do you fix your breakfast—make the coffee or toast first? Do you brush your teeth before you floss or vice versa? And then there are our habitual thoughts. Ugh, the ongoing monologue.

Changing our habits takes time. We first have to change our words. "Change your words, change your world." For example, what we tell ourselves when we delay working out affects our motivation: "it hurts" or "it's fun!" Yes, it takes time and commitment and as with any change you want to make, you need to start a new routine slowly. You take the first step and then another, and soon, you begin to feel the mental benefits and see the physical effects.

It's the same with organizing our space—it takes time and commitment, and sometimes, it hurts. We don't want to hurt; we don't want to be in pain ever. If you begin with a box of items that hold painful memories, you will not say, "Ooh! Sign me up!" Most people give up at that point, even in this early stage. They think every box will be like this— painful, messy, and difficult to process. Trust in your strength. It will be painful, but you are now more aware of the possibility of improvement.

Let's go back to the fitness analogy. You wouldn't begin a new fitness routine by running five miles—especially if you haven't exercised in a while. Instead, you might start with a checkup, join a gym or and hire a personal trainer to create a personalized routine. My "why" in my organizing business is to help you create a new way of thinking about the change you want to make in your space. Then we create a personalized solution that will help you become organized. You must be committed to the new habit of staying organized, just like with a workout for staying healthier.

Uncomfortable at times? Out of your comfort zone, for sure. Worth it? You tell me.

17
Spatulas

Chapter Twenty-Nine

The Myths We Tell Ourselves

*If we change our words, we can change our world. This
means that if we change our inner stories and ideas
about ourselves, we can also change our bodies.*
—Andrea Gardner, *Change Your Words, Change Your World*

"What are the myths you tell yourself?"

I looked at the mindset coach at the front of the room. I was at a weekend retreat in a workshop with about a hundred others. I didn't understand what she was talking about until she continued asking questions.

"What's holding you back from achieving the next level in your life or your business? What makes you feel like you don't stand out from the crowd? Why do you think you're not successful in landing more business? Or meeting that special someone?"

My two workshop partners and I discussed this question at length, and I realized there was a huge myth I didn't even know I had held onto since my teen years.

When the coach asked for volunteers to share their experience, I went directly to the microphone in the audience: "Well, I'm pretty average at just about everything. Average looking, average height, average talent, average smarts."

The coach looked confused, then explained. "Lisa, from the times I've seen and heard from you this weekend, I can see that you are anything but average!"

My fellow attendees murmured their agreement.

My chest tightened, and I breathed through a sudden well of tears. My turn to explain. "I don't know why, but for the last thirty-five years, I've lived my life thinking and accepting that I'm average, that there is nothing special or unique about me." It was this revelation that led to a deeper dive and a huge transformation that weekend. As in my experience with my ex-boyfriend, I hadn't realized how much this false belief had held me back and stopped me from taking risks and excelling in my life, relationships, and business.

When I was a dancer, I didn't have the confidence to try out for the lead roles because to be the star, I would have to stand out. So, what would I, believing I am average, choose? Exactly, not to stand out—I made sure I looked like everyone else, and then they would pick me for the chorus, and I would be able to at least perform in the show.

This myth I held about myself also fed into others. For example, in my marriage, I was convinced that my husband should make all the decisions—including all the financial ones—because he was the man and the primary breadwinner. I also felt he was the smart one, and I was not. I think my undiagnosed and untreated ADD exacerbated these myths. He also likes a lot of structure, and I dislike it, even as an organizer. I never read directions, and I am more of a go-with-the-flow person.

These myths I had about myself were not helping; they hindered my life and marriage. However, once I was aware of them and acknowledged they were false, I felt more confident and looked at myself differently.

What are some of the myths you tell yourself? For example, you may think, "I am not organized. My home will never be perfect, like in the pictures." Or you say to yourself, "I will never be able to do this." In your relationships? "I'll never be married because no one likes me enough. I'm not worthy of love."

Take a look at those myths and see how they hold you back. How much of an energy drain are they without you even knowing it? Once you are aware of the myths, decide whether they work for you. If they do not, challenge those myths and see how you grow—as a person and in your professional life.

You are not "the story" that you tell yourself. We often connect our identity with myths about our accomplishments, past events, and heartaches, and we get stuck there. While all the events in your life culminate in who you are today, you are not the myths.

I hope you navigate the gap from where you are to where you want to be.

17
Spatulas

Chapter Thirty

The Man Who Fried an Egg

By the time the leaves had begun to change, we had completed a full declutter of the basement, the entire first floor, and the upstairs guest room. Finally, we were both ready to tackle the main bedroom together—where his heart had died. Standing in the doorway, I picked up a huge plastic tub full of dog items. Kita's puppy bowl, small collar, and leash lay on the balls, chew toys, and unopened bags of food and treats.

"Just give it all away. Throw it out. I don't care," Vince mumbled faintly.

My heart broke.

"Vince, if it were that easy, you would have already done that."

"You're right. It's not the answer. I would always wonder what was lost. Okay, what do you suggest?"

"I think we can agree that I can donate much of the stuff, put a lot of these old newspapers and magazines into a box for recycling and keep adding to the garbage bag, right?"

He nodded, watching me, and then looked around the crowded room. I could feel his confidence in my leadership and how trust replaced his earlier embarrassment. He trusted that with my help, we were finding our way through the tatters of his life.

"Great, so let's set up a station in the other bedroom for you with these empty boxes, one for keepers, one for recycling, and one for donation. While I work here discarding old newspapers and magazines and recycling and getting the garbage out, I will bring boxes of items out for you to go through."

Eventually, Vince looked through everything. He had me donate the dog items to an animal shelter and full grocery bags of other things we uncovered to the thrift store.

"What a great day, Mrs. Rigoni, don't you think?" He took a deep breath watching me work from where he stood outside the doorway.

"Well, yes, I do, Mr. P." I grinned and kept working.

This third session upstairs was when he was finally ready to go inside The Room. We had created enough space so when he gave me a wink, I brought in the chair and small table from the other room, and we got to work. He didn't say much; he just took what I put in front of him, made decisions, and moved on to the next item. I could feel the residual sadness, though, so I made sure to give him easy things for decisions. Again, he worked hard to stay focused on each task.

"She took what she wanted and left while I was at work. I never saw it coming."

Her side of the closet and dresser were still set up the same way as the day she left. He hadn't touched anything in nine years.

I put her jewelry and small items into a box for Vince to go through.

"Yep, she took all the good stuff I bought her." He sighed. "Just donate the rest. I don't want it here anymore."

The bathroom connected to the main bedroom was like every other room: boxes and loose items stacked high, pushed and crammed, heaved and thrown inside so I could not get in. There wasn't an inch of space left for anything more.

"This whole room became a disaster zone to try and forget, to seal in all the terrible memories of my ex-wife and the painful events of that time." Vince sighed. "But what I did was cut off my life and block any of the good memories." He chuckled. "There were a few."

Vince took the plunge and started in the connected bathroom, grabbing items and making decisions even before I saw them in his hands—he was handing things to me for the garbage! By now, he realized how cathartic and freeing it was for him. "I am not the same person I was when all this took place," he told me.

I shook my head in response. "No, Vince, you are not. You are not the same person I met seven months ago. And I have learned a great deal from you about resilience, determination, and strength. I have watched you work through the pain, fear, and uncertainty."

Vince is very logical, and the absurdity of the stuff he saved made no rational sense. Bottles of soy nut butter, new, unopened packs of underwear, hundreds of highlighter pens, tins of tuna fish. One day, he started laughing at what he found, which got me laughing, pretty much doing us in for the day!

"I love to hear you laugh, Vince," I said, wiping the tears from my eyes.

"Ha, me too. It's with your help, Lisa, it's with your help." Then, he gave me a lazy grin. "This whole situation is quite ridiculous when you think about it. Paying someone to help me throw stuff out that I don't remember needing, wanting, or even buying in the first place. How can it be so hard? But it is."

When we finished clearing out the main bedroom, Vince was a transformed man from the one I had met months earlier. He kept looking better, and his steps were lighter. Vince finally understood why he was holding onto things from the past and how they did not serve him anymore. Taking on the challenging work of facing his past had freed him from it. He even looked younger, gentler, and at peace with himself in a new way.

During all those hours we spent together, we laughed, cried, and shared a lot. He had a fascinating past yet couldn't see a future for himself. He shared all the areas in his life he wished he would have done more, had more confidence in himself, and spoken up for himself. He had two sons, who he would drive and visit as often as possible, and grandchildren. But, until we worked together, he would not allow them to come and visit him.

Vince was also an avid swimmer and he couldn't do it anymore because of his injuries. Even still, it was a goal of his to get back in the pool someday. My daughter was also a competitive swimmer at the time, and we often talked about that, and he would give me tips for her. He gave her a towel and a book at one point. He wanted to hear all about her progress and loved when I shared her times after she had a swim meet.

———————————

My mother had been sick during the seven months Vince and I worked together. Each time I traveled to Chicago to visit her, I saw her getting frailer, and her dementia increased. Nevertheless, my mom and I enjoyed being together, having time to sit and talk, laugh, cry, and say everything we wanted and needed to say to each other. Each time I returned to Virginia and met with Vince, he always asked how the family was and especially how Mom was doing. I would give him the update while he proudly showed me his homework, and then we would be on with the task for that session.

———————————

On November 5, 2014, eight months since our first meeting, I arrived at Vince's, exhausted from yet another late flight from Chicago and being at my mother's bedside. Although I was tired and grief had kept me awake most of the night, I was not going to let Vince down, and I wanted something to distract me from the pain in my heart.

"Hi, Lisa!" Vince's expected big grin and positive energy greeted me when he answered my knock at 10 in the morning.

"Hey, Vince. How are you doing today? Ready to finish that storage room?"

He nodded, his recently styled thick gray hair bobbing, light blue eyes twinkling with life and hope, and his energy high. Complete 180 from the shell of the man he had been.

I smiled back, swallowing past the lump of grief lodged in my throat.

We worked side by side for a bit. While he did most of the work, this new Vince soon noticed the sadness I couldn't hide.

"How was your trip to Chicago?" he asked quietly, searching my eyes, which were quickly tearing up.

I glanced down for a moment. "It was good. I got to see my mom." I paused, biting my lip to keep from busting.

Vince moved closer and wrapped his arm around me.

I patted his hand and blew out a breath. "She's gone, Vince. Right after Marinna and I touched down at Dulles. And I knew—" I looked away; my pain raw. "—I knew when my brother texted me to call him as soon as I got home." Then I looked Vince in the eyes. "She wanted to make sure we got home safely before she could join my dad. Loving and protective Mama until her last breath."

Vince and I were both crying, and now it was difficult for me to meet his gaze.

"What are you doing here, Lisa? Go home and be with your family. You don't need to worry about me."

I shook my head. "Thank you, Vince. You don't know how much being here and having you to come and work with has helped me today."

He wrapped me in a tight hug and started walking me out.

"No, wait, Vince, we have work to do here. Let's finish up. My mom and dad taught me always to keep my word, even when it's difficult. This time it is not."

He nodded, and we got back to work.

By Thanksgiving, Vince was satisfied with the project for his townhouse. No need for protection or comfort from stuff anymore. He would need to sort through and donate a couple of things, but he was happy and peaceful, which was the ultimate goal.

I purchased a small Christmas tree; one Sunday my husband, daughter, and I brought it over to him. We'd gone through his whole house, so I knew he didn't have anything Christmassy.

As we admired his new tree, we shared some hugs and a few more tears. We had both grown so much during our time together. When I first arrived, I was confident I could get the job done as I do for any project. In a flash, though, I had doubted my competency, strength, and dedication to assist.

Vince's situation gave me the gift of introspection to find deeper courage for my work with myself and my clients. I had witnessed Vince come back to life. He now enjoyed time more, both inside and outside his home. He even invited friends over for dinner and put together his profile on a dating app. His boys and their families were coming for Christmas. We had both profoundly changed from when we met on his front porch in what seemed years earlier.

When you hold space for yourself, you can hold space for others. I genuinely believe Vince could not have been there for me in my time of grief (nor would I have wanted to be with him the morning after my mother passed) if he hadn't cleared enough space for himself—his heart was open to let others in again, to let me in. And he became more than a client I helped; Vince is a friend who also helped me—to grow.

Vince was also instrumental in my rebrand. Soon after finishing the project with him, I realized the process and the intensity at which he had grown was much more than "just" organizing and clearing material items. Healing happened. He reclaimed his life along with his space.

Digging through the emotional stuff transforms us on a cellular level. Client after client tells me that they feel mentally and physically clearer through what I have taught them. They learn new ways to live, think about their stuff, and understand why they hold on to some items or have lost connection with other things in their home. As a result, many have found stronger and deeper relationships within themselves and others.

That is the origin of The Organizing Mentors. More than organizing physical belongings, we are about digging deep to reclaim physical and mental space.

The acknowledgment opens the door to Becoming.
—Kim Radke

Throughout the months of our working together, Vince continued sessions with his therapist, and we would do regular check-ins, the three of us. He ended our final group session by phone, saying, "I feel such love and support. I don't know how I deserve it." We shared so much through those months that I came to think of him as an older brother and a friend. I felt privileged to witness him become more confident, less anxious, and oh, that smile! He was breathing easier, walking straighter, and looking younger. His transformation was—magical.

———————

Just before the holidays, my phone rang at 8:15 in the morning.

"Gooooood morning, Lisa." Unmistakably, Vince's super-energized voice was in my ear.

"Vince, is everything okay? How much coffee have you had already?"

He was bursting to share something with me. "Ha, I'm drinking decaf now. I want you to know that I ate a great breakfast this morning. And it wasn't cereal and milk."

I smiled, excited for him. "Did you go out with someone?" I thought he was telling me he had a date.

"Nope, even better than a date with a woman. I had a date with myself in my kitchen." He paused. "I fried an egg in *my* kitchen on my new stove." Then, his voice quivering, he said, "I haven't been able to do that in over eight years."

I couldn't speak. Neither of us could. We both started crying and then laughed—at the ridiculousness, amazingness, and beauty.

"Was it good, Vince?"

"Best fried egg I've ever had!"

Many clients have made beautiful, life-changing, and empowering testimonials about how they have recovered their space mentally and physically—moving on with their lives and in their homes with less clutter. However, I have to say that the most incredible words I have ever heard are, for sure, "I fried an egg in my kitchen for the first time in over eight years."

17
Spatulas

Chapter Thirty-One

The Stuff About Your Stuff
is not About Your Stuff

*One day you will tell your story of how you overcame what you
went through and it will be someone else's survival guide.*
—Brené Brown

Everyone has clutter. Some of it we can see in our homes, cars, and offices. And some clutter we walk around with daily, deep inside where no one can see, not even us.

I started my journey into professional organizing in 2008. Little did I know that in 2006 when I discovered I had ADD, organizing would become my business. During my childhood, teens, and adult life, I would sort things from small to tall or by color or category. The exercise calmed me, gave my space a more serene look, and gave me something other than the chaos around me to focus on when it was too much for me. (I didn't have a name for it back then, but it was organizing.)

Some of the chaos was external, such as too much noise, stuff, and even overpowering odors. Too many people, loud voices, and loud music would affect me. My internal chaos came from in-my-head overthinking and reviewing scenarios about what I wish I had said or could have done—also procrastinating or going over everything I needed to do. In some situations, I didn't have enough confidence to follow through or believe I could be perfect, so why even try? I would also hold onto negative comments from someone years before that I just couldn't forget.

We all hold on to old habits and thoughts for many reasons. Sometimes I am afraid of change, and I like staying in my comfort zone, or I'm not even aware that the old habits and thoughts are holding me back. Therapists say we only hold onto these thoughts and behaviors because they serve us somehow—we get a charge, a benefit, and even a thrill. So how does holding on to too much stuff, mentally and physically, serve us today? What is the payoff in holding onto fears, past mistakes, vendettas, and false beliefs?

Through therapy, digging deep into my past, and almost two decades as a professional organizer, I realized that everyone I meet, no matter how successful, happy, busy, or alone one is, everyone has stuff. And everyone has a story about their stuff that has nothing to do with their physical stuff. (Read that sentence until you get it.)

In my office at this very moment, I have a large moving box filled to the brim with stamps. My brothers and I found dozens of oversized manila envelopes overflowing with little see-through plastic envelopes filled with stamps, cigar boxes with old war stamps, wildlife, and states of the United States collections. There are binders full of stamps sealed in plastic in very special cardboard folders and postcards and letters with stamps on them from a time when you didn't have to put a return address on the envelope. Can you believe that? My mom's father and my dad shared the joy of stamp collecting. My grandfather lived in Washington state, and my dad in Illinois. They sent hundreds of letters back and forth because, in the '60s, '70s, and '80s, that's how they would share their latest find. My grandpa also sent funny cartoons, silly cards, and copies of dirty, crass drawings that I remember my dad roaring over for hours. They shared a special bond. The two of them also shared a very deep love for my mom and each other.

My grandpa would visit us every September and bring a small suitcase full of stamps, and, with my dad, they would spend hours exploring and organizing the piles of stamps on the dining room table. He came to visit in September because he, my mom, and his ex-wife (my grandma) shared birthdays and their wedding anniversary that month. It seemed a little odd to me (but my family is a little odd) that they wanted to spend their wedding anniversary together since they divorced in 1938. It was also magical, sweet, and truly wonderful to know how much they still loved and admired each other, even though they weren't married. If they had stayed married, they would have celebrated their 69th anniversary in 1997, when my grandpa passed away. Was this little hobby of theirs an obsession? It's difficult to say. But the fact that my house now contains tens of thousands of stamps may be the proof.

I know I have been holding on to the stamp collection to keep my father's and grandpa's love for each other alive. And I know that is not logical because their love will never die, even though they have both passed away. I guess it's a way for me to feel close to them and to be a part of their little world that they shared.

Writing this book made me aware of many things I was holding on to that I hadn't realized. Once I was aware, I could not go back. So, I had to make a choice: Do I ignore what I know or make a change? I've written this book to challenge you: Do you want to make a change and stop keeping secrets from yourself as to why you hold on to things or continue to ignore your truth?

When I realized why I was holding on to the stamp collection, I searched for a stamp collector. Keeping this massive box of stamps would not bring my loved ones back, and releasing it would not remove their love or memories from me.

We must dig deep and be honest with ourselves when making a change. While it's not easy, it is simple.

Chapter Thirty-Two

Coming Full Circle

*Twenty years from now, you will be more disappointed by
the things you didn't do than by the ones you did. So, throw
off the bowlines. Sail away from the safe harbor.
Catch the winds of your sails. Explore. Dream. Discover.*
—Mark Twain

At the end of June 2021, my family and I headed to Chicago to wrap up the process of selling my childhood home. My hubby and I would stay at the house with my middle brother, Paul, who had moved into our childhood home four years after my dad died. Paul kept an eye on Mom as she became frailer physically and her dementia worsened. Our youngest brother, Vic, and his family lived nearby, and our oldest brother, Drew, with his family, stayed with them.

We were all there for a family wedding, after which Drew and I had planned to stay an extra week to help wrap up loose ends, get the remaining items out of the house, and then put the house up for sale. Instead, we spent a whole month because there was still so much to do. Many of the items my brothers and I thought we would want to keep when the house sold turned out to be less important. So, I researched and found some local charities where we could donate the remaining furniture and housewares. I was confident I could accomplish things because that's what I do.

However, I was unprepared for how emotionally taxing and draining it would be.

This house, this hub, the rock of my childhood, would soon no longer be in my family. This part of my story was over, and I would no longer stay there when I visited—no more access to the fabulous backyard or enjoying the cuttings from the flowers my mom planted 45 years before, sitting on the stone planter my grandfather built, or going inside to sit in my childhood bedroom again.

For four weeks, I woke up early in the morning, did work for my business, made some calls, and then hit the ground running, taking care of things to get the house ready to go. Paul left early for work, and Drew and Vic would come over mid-afternoon with some lunch. After that, all three of us would continue with the checklist, run errands and drop off donations. Then, Paul would return around 5, and get to work packing his things to move out. Finally, my sister-in-law, Michelle, would bring dinner around 8, after her full workday. Dinner usually included a glass of wine or two and always a good laugh or a needed cry from a story someone shared.

Most nights, when we had the energy, we would continue until midnight. My brothers and I painted, cleaned, and fixed things; I used toothbrushes to deep-clean the bathrooms; we changed light bulbs and fixtures, caulked and glued, wiped, and shined. We took down the drop ceiling in the basement and tiled a new floor. We invested time and money to ensure that the house expressed all the love, support, and history that it represented to us. We wanted to make our parents proud and our grandparents too, who invested their time, money, and energy into building this house. Up to the last week, we found more items stashed in hidden spots around the basement and attic.

Selling all those items was another stressful part because we wanted our parents' precious belongings to go to nice people. And, for the most part, the universe chose the right people. The best part of selling our parents' things was that my best friend Sheila, from kindergarten, who I stayed in touch with, bought my parents' dining room table and chairs. She saw it posted for sale and remembered all the love, laughter, and memories we shared around that table, where she joined us many times. It's now in her home, creating new memories for her family.

We found it difficult to see our parents' items leave "their" home. And going through this process myself increased the empathy I have for my clients and how hard it is for them when we sell their belongings.

We decided to have our last family dinner in the house the night before my daughter and I left. We ordered some takeout, and my sister-in-law and I set my parents' dining room table with paper plates, paper napkins, wine glasses, and candles. Then, we face-timed my husband, brother-in-law, and nephew, who were back home. Finally, we toasted our parents, each other, and the love we shared in that house and around that table for 55 years.

The following morning, when I was about to leave our family home for the last time, my thoughts were frantic, manic. "This is the last time I will walk down the hall, use this sink, the bathroom, and the shower." I walked around every room, touched every windowsill, talking to my parents the whole time. Then, finally, I went downstairs and sat in my little cubby between the wall and the bar that was my place of refuge and comfort for many years while I was young.

I had to leave to make my flight, so when I closed the door and walked out of the house one last time, I was bawling my eyes out but with a smile.

A few days later, we closed on the house, and my brother Vic took one final video of the whole house before they locked the door, and our family home became someone else's to love.

I'm a true believer that things happen the way they are supposed to. But, of course, sometimes we don't know why or how and can't make sense of why events occur the way they do. I truly believe my parents had something to do with the new owners. We found out that a great family bought the house. From when we were growing up, the neighbors who lived across the street from us now had kids our age. The wife had passed away, and years later, the husband remarried. The new owner is the granddaughter of his second wife. We couldn't have asked for anything better.

Knowing in my heart how much my family and our memories in that house kept us happy for so long and made me who I am, helped me release my family home and items.

There's a great interview with Stephen Colbert and Anderson Cooper where Anderson asked Stephen if he really believes that "You need to love the thing you most wish didn't happen." And Stephen said, "Yes." And he then added, "What punishments of God are not gifts? It's a gift to exist. It's a gift to exist and with existence comes suffering. There is no escaping that." Stephen believes this truth he has also heard said in Catholic and Buddhist traditions. "If you are grateful for your life, really grateful for your life, you can't pick and choose what you're grateful for. You have to be grateful for all of it. The good, the bad, the ugly, the painful, and the exhausting."

I am so grateful for all the love and lessons I learned in that little house on Homestead Road—all the memories and experiences, positive and negative, that I've accumulated and tucked away. Those early days of organizing the bathroom linen closet and hiding in my cubby in the basement shaped me into the woman I am today and made it possible for me to extend my empathy, love, and knowledge to my clients and now you, my reader.

Thank you for being part of this journey.

Acknowledgments

This book is what it is with a warm appreciation for my three writing angels: Michelle, Lynn, and Drew. Thank you, thank you, thank you.

Michelle A. Gil, author of *Don't Tell Me to Get Over It, A Memoir of Love and Loss,* is a beautiful writer, poet, and storyteller. She is one of my original writing group members and supported me in the developmental editing of the first 17 versions.

My copy editor, Lynn Thompson, Living on Purpose Communications, took 17 parts of my rough manuscript and condensed them into a single rough draft that I could polish and tweak. Then, a year later, after more review with Michelle, I returned to Lynn for intensive collaboration in preparation for publishing. You are reading this book today because of Lynn's brilliance.

My brother, Drew, a professional writer for Broadway, was an invaluable source of support, especially when mining childhood memories. And oh, we recalled some delicious stories together.

My brothers, Paul and Vic, recalled intricate details from our childhood that I had forgotten, bringing all our celebrations back to life.

Three of the original four men in my life reinforced my strength to tell the story of how I experienced life on Homestead Road. We all lived there together in love, laughter, and chaos, and I am forever grateful for all our years together (and they're not over yet).

Thanks a million, to the writing mentors I reached out to for HELP! My two high school buddies are Terry Banker, author of *Conquering Cancer*, and Chris Westfall, author of *The New Elevator Pitch* and *Easier.* Your insight, guidance, and humor were everything and more than I could ask for on this journey.

Warm appreciation to William Lodge. Thank you for coming into my life.

Thank you to my brother-in-law, Bill Randall, US Naval Intelligence Officer (1630), for helping me with military descriptions.

Jason Rufner with *The Semantic Stylist* was my first writing partner, helping me put into words The LITL System.

Thank you to all my intelligent and knowledgeable friends and partners for granting me interview time in their busy schedules. Warm appreciation for Cyndi Turner, LCSW, LSATP, MAC, author of *Can I Keep Drinking? How You Can Decide When Enough Is Enough,* and Craig James, LCSW, LSATP, MAC, Co-Founders of Insight into Action Therapy; Tamara Wolfe, of Full Spectrum Living, Certified Life Coach, Speaker, Author, and Trainer, Certified NeuroCoach and NeuroLeader; Cindy Battino, CEO of Transformational Healing, and Dianne Andruzzi, MSW, LCSW. I appreciate you making sure I was moving along on the right track.

Thanks to my beta readers who gave me valuable insights and feedback: Cindy Battino, Cyndi Turner, Dianne Andruzzi, Heidi Roed, Sue Gilad, Tamara Wolfe, and Terry Banker.

Thank you to Becky Norwood of Spotlight Publishing House for your calm guidance, fantastic expertise, and encouraging confidence in bringing my book to publication. I appreciate your patience with my process of sharing these stories in the way I knew I could tell them.

A huge thank you bouquet for the Loud and Clear Marketing Team—Deborah Haynes Swider, Sharon Wright, Kristi Quill, Katie Raicea, Krissy Davies, and Derek Archer, for all the social media and website support behind the scenes. You are a fantastic cheering section and kept me going despite myself!

Starting my business was me alone, and I needed more assistance as my client list quickly grew. I want to thank all the incredible women who have worked with me since 2009: Ginny Mamatas, Marie-Therese Rancourt, Victoria Willett, Camille Sweger, Kathleen Ortt, Libby Crangle, Danielle Gofran, Barbara Houhoulis, Karen Merchant, Dena Fleisher, Debbie Hobson, Nancy Femrite, Chris Hunn, Becca Sipes, and Sally Prouty. Sally has been my right-hand gal since 2016! Thank you all for helping our clients transform their organizational struggles from chaos to calm.

And a warm thank you to Aunt Joan Haynes Latham for your perfect spatula for my book cover.

I credit my success with the compilation of my business, this book, and my wonderful life thanks to my accepting, supportive, and understanding husband, Gene, and my beautiful daughter, Marinna, who, at 19, is more self-aware than I may ever be. They have encouraged me for the last two years during this tremendous undertaking. It became a thing in our house: "Okay, well, time for me to go work on my book. You guys enjoy the movie," and "Sorry, no, you guys eat without me. I am working on my book," and "Did you know my mom is writing a book?" Their patience and love allowed me to sit undisturbed at my desk evenings and weekends to get this book out to you.

Trust and know that, with organization,
you will get your life back (and a book written).
—Lisa Geraci Rigoni

17"
Spatulas

About the Author

Lisa Geraci Rigoni is the owner and CDO (Chief Declutter Officer) of The Organizing Mentors, a company specializing in home organization and move management, and is a certified company with The National Association of Senior & Specialty Move Managers. Lisa has been helping her clients reclaim their space mentally and physically since 2008. She and her team assist clients in the Northern Virginia and Washington DC areas with various services, including relocation, sorting, and purging. In 2020, The Organizing Mentors went worldwide with the addition of virtual organizing.

Beyond organizing space, Lisa and her Team Mentors empower their clients and inspire confidence to make positive choices that enrich their lives and set them free from the habits that have kept their minds and spaces cluttered.

As an advocate, philanthropist, and champion for non-profits in her area, especially Habitat for Humanity, Lisa was one of the determined and committed women helping to establish Women Giving Back (www.womengivingback.org) as the beacon of hope it is today for women and children in crisis. A much sought-after speaker, mentor, and author, Lisa lives in Northern Virginia with her husband, daughter, and fur baby Sadie Belle. Lisa loves working out, exploring Virginia wine country, and making the most of every day.

Keep in touch with Lisa Geraci Rigoni

**We welcome hearing from you
with your questions, success stories,
and Amazon reviews of**
17 Spatulas and the Man Who Fried an Egg:
Reclaim Your Space Mentally and Physically

If you learned something from the introduction to The LITL System, my next book is a deeper dive LITL workbook that will take you through each step to help you create the changes you desire. Also, when you sign up for my newsletter, I will notify you of release dates and events where I'll be speaking.

www.theorganizingmentors.com

Printed in the USA
CPSIA information can be obtained
at www.ICGtesting.com
LVHW011645011123
762773LV00005B/25

9 781958 405598